ISEE® PREP

Independent School Entrance Exam Study Guide
and Practice Test Questions

COPYRIGHT

Copyright © 2025 by Complete Test Preparation Inc.
ALL RIGHTS RESERVED. No part of this book may be r reproduced or transferred in any form or by any means, graphic, electronic, or mechanical, including photocopying, recording, web distribution, taping, or by any information storage retrieval system, without the written permission of the author.

Notice: Complete Test Preparation Inc. makes every reasonable effort to obtain from reliable sources accurate, complete, and timely information about the tests covered in this book. Nevertheless, changes can be made in the tests or the administration of the tests at any time and Complete Test Preparation Inc. makes no representation or warranty, either expressed or implied as to the accuracy, timeliness, or completeness of the information contained in this book. Complete Test Preparation Inc. makes no representations or warranties of any kind, express or implied, about the completeness, accuracy, reliability, suitability or availability with respect to the information contained in this document for any purpose. Any reliance you place on such information is therefore strictly at your own risk.

The author(s) shall not be liable for any loss incurred as a consequence of the use and application, directly or indirectly, of any information presented in this work. Sold with the understanding, the author(s) is not engaged in rendering professional services or advice. If advice or expert assistance is required, the services of a competent professional should be sought.

The company, product and service names used in this publication are for identification purposes only. All trademarks and registered trademarks are the property of their respective owners. Complete Test Preparation Inc. is not affiliated with any educational institution.

ISEE® and the Independent School Entrance Exam are registered trademarks of Educational Records Bureau, who are not involved in the production of, and do not endorse this publication.

We strongly recommend that students check with exam providers for up-to-date information regarding test content.

Published by
Complete Test Preparation Inc.
Victoria BC Canada V8S 4H9
Visit us on the web at https://www.test-preparation.ca
Printed in the USA

About Complete Test Preparation Inc.

Why Us?
The Complete Test Preparation Team has been publishing high quality study materials since 2005, with a catalogue of over 145 titles, in English, French and Chinese, as well as ESL curriculum for all levels.

To keep up with the industry changes, we update everything all the time!

And the best part?
With every purchase, you're helping people all over the world improve themselves and their education. So thank you in advance for supporting this mission with us! Together, we are truly making a difference in the lives of those often forgotten by the system.

Charities that we support
https://www.test-preparation.ca/charities-and-non-profits/

You have definitely come to the right place.
If you want to spend your valuable study time where it will help you the most - we've got you covered today and tomorrow.

ISBN-13: 978-1-77245-506-9

Version 9 June 2025

Contents

6 Getting Started
- How this study guide is organized — 6
- The ISEE® Study Plan — 7
- Making a Study Schedule — 8
- Tips for making a schedule — 11

12 Verbal Reasoning
- Verbal Reasoning Self-Assessment — 13
- Answer Key — 18

20 Quantitative Reasoning
- Quantitative Reasoning Self-Assessment — 21
- Answer Key — 26

27 Reading Comprehension
- Reading Self-Assessment — 28
- Answer Key — 38
- Help with Reading Comprehension — 41
- Main Idea and Supporting Details — 43
- Drawing Inferences And Conclusions — 46

49 Mathematics
- Math Self-Assessment — 52
- Answer Key — 57
- How to Solve Word Problems — 61
- Types of Word Problems — 63
- Fraction Tips, Tricks and Shortcuts — 69
- Decimal Tips, Tricks and Shortcuts — 72
- Percent Tips, Tricks and Shortcuts — 73
- How to Answer Basic Math Multiple Choice — 74

78 How to Write an Essay
- Example Essay 1 — 79
- Example Essay 2 — 82
- Example Essay 3 — 84
- Example Essay Prompts — 87
- Common Essay Mistakes Example I — 88
- Common Essay Mistakes Example II — 89
- Writing Concisely — 91

- 93 Practice Test Questions Set 1
  Answer Key 130
- 145 Practice Test Questions Set 2
  Answer Key 179
- 193 What to Do After Taking a Practice Test
- 196 Conclusion
- 197 Online Resources

Getting Started

CONGRATULATIONS! By deciding to take the Independent School Entrance Exam (ISEE®), you have taken the first step toward a great future! Of course, there is no point in taking this important examination unless you intend to do your best to earn the highest grade you possibly can. That means getting yourself organized and discovering the best approaches, methods and strategies to master the material. Yes, that will require real effort and dedication on your part but if you are willing to focus your energy and devote the study time necessary, before you know it you will be on you way to a brighter future!

We know that taking on a new endeavour can be a little scary, and it is easy to feel unsure of where to begin. That's where we come in. This study guide is designed to help you improve your test-taking skills, show you a few tricks of the trade and increase both your competency and confidence.

The Independent School Entrance Exam

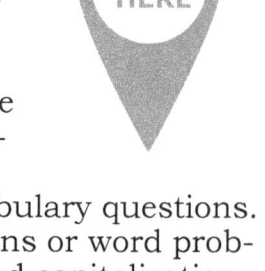

The ISEE® exam is composed of five sections, verbal reasoning, quantitative skills, reading, mathematics and language skills. The verbal reasoning section consists of analogies, synonyms and antonyms, logic and verbal classification. The quantitative skills section consists of number series, geometric and non geometric comparisons, and basic math. The reading section consists of reading comprehension and vocabulary questions. The mathematics section consists of problem solving questions or word problems. The language skills section consists of punctuation and capitalization, English usage, spelling and composition.

While we seek to make our guide as comprehensive as possible, note that like all exams, the ISEE® Exam might be adjusted at some future point. New material might be added, or content that is no longer relevant or applicable might be removed. It is always a good idea to give the materials you receive when you register to take the ISEE® a careful review.

How this study guide is organized

This study guide is divided into three sections. The first section, Self-Assessments, which will help you recognize your areas of strength and weaknesses. This will be a boon when it comes to managing your study time most efficiently; there is not much point of focusing on material you have already got firmly under control. Instead, taking the self-assessments will show you where that time could be much better spent. In this area you will begin with a few questions to quickly evaluate your understanding of material that is likely to appear on the ISEE®. If you do poorly in certain areas, simply work carefully through those sections in the tutorials and then try the self-assessment again.

The second section, Tutorials, offers information in each of the content areas, as well as strategies to help you master that material. The tutorials are not intended to be a complete course, but cover general principles. If you find that you do not understand the tutorials, it is recommended that you seek out additional instruction.

Third, we offer two sets of practice test questions, similar to those on the ISEE® Exam.

The ISEE® Study Plan

Now that you have made the decision to take the ISEE®, it is time to get started. Before you do another thing, you will need to figure out a plan of attack. The very best study tip is to start early! The longer the time period you devote to regular study practice, the more likely you will retain the material and be able to access it quickly. If you thought that 1x20 is the same as 2x10, guess what? It really is not, when it comes to study time. Reviewing material for just an hour per day over the course of 20 days is far better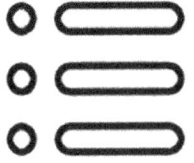
than studying for two hours a day for only 10 days. The more often you revisit a particular piece of information, the better you will know it. Not only will your grasp and understanding be better, but your ability to reach into your brain and quickly and efficiently pull out the tidbit you need, will be greatly enhanced as well.

The great Chinese scholar and philosopher Confucius believed that true knowledge could be defined as knowing both what you know and what you do not know. The first step in preparing for the ISEE® is to assess your strengths and weaknesses. You may already have an idea of what you know and what you do not know, but evaluating yourself using our Self- Assessment modules for each of the three areas, Math, Writing and Quantitative skills, will clarify the details.

Making a Study Schedule

To make your study time most productive you will need to develop a study plan. The purpose of the plan is to organize all the bits of pieces of information in such a way that you will not feel overwhelmed. Rome was not built in a day, and learning everything you will need to know to pass the ISEE® is going to take time, too. Arranging the material you need to learn into manageable chunks is the best way to go. Each study session should make you feel as though you have succeeded in accomplishing your goal, and your goal is simply to learn what you planned to learn during that particular session. Try to organize the content in such a way that each study session builds on previous ones. That way, you will retain the information, be better able to access it, and review the previous bits and pieces at the same time.

Self-assessment

The Best Study Tip! The very best study tip is to start early! The longer you study regularly, the more you will retain and 'learn' the material. Studying for 1 hour per day for 20 days is far better than studying for 2 hours for 10 days.

What don't you know?

The first step is to assess your strengths and weaknesses. You may already have an idea of where your weaknesses are, or you can take our Self-assessment modules for each of the content areas.

Exam Component	Rate 1 to 5
Verbal Reasoning	
Synonyms	
Sentence Completion	
Quantitative Reasoning	
Problem Solving	
Quantitative Comparison	
Mathematics	
Arithmetic	
Algebra	
Geometry	
Reading Comprehension	

Making a Study Schedule

The key to making a study plan is to divide the material you need to learn into manageable sized pieces and learn it, while at the same time reviewing the material that you already know.

Using the table above, any scores of 3 or below, you need to spend time learning, going over and practicing this subject area. A score of 4 means you need to review the material, but you don't have to spend time re-learning. A score of 5 and you are OK with just an occasional review before the exam. A score of 0 or 1 means you really need to work on this should allocate the most time and the highest priority. Some students prefer a 5-day plan and others a 10-day plan. It also depends on how much time you have until the exam.

Here is an example of a 5-day plan based on an example from the table above:

Synonyms: 1- Study 1 hour everyday – review on last day

Quantitative Comparisons: 3 - Study 1 hour for 3 days then ½ hour a day, then review

Problem Solving (Word Problems): 4 - Review every second day

Geometric Comparison: 2 - Study 1 hour first day – then ½ hour everyday

Algebra: 5 - Review for ½ hour every other day

Reading Comp.: 5 - Review for ½ hour every other day

Using this example, reading comprehension and algebra are good and only need occasional review. Geometric Comparison is good and needs 'some' review. Quantitative Comparisons needs a bit of work, Word Problems need a lot of work and Synonyms are very weak and need the most time. Based on this, here is a sample study plan:

Day	Subject	Time
Monday		
Study	Synonyms	1 hour
Study	Word Problems	1 hour
½ hour break		
Study	Quantitative Comparisons	1 hour
Review	Reading Comp.	½ hour
Tuesday		
Study	Synonyms	1 hour
Study	Word Problems	½ hour
½ hour break		
Study	Quantitative Comparisons	½ hour
Review	Algebra	½ hour
Review	Reading Comp.	½ hour
Wednesday		
Study	Synonyms	1 hour
Study	Word Problems	½ hour
½ hour break		
Study	Quantitative Comparisons	½ hour
Review	Reading Comp.	½ hour
Thursday		
Study	Synonyms	½ hour
Study	Word Problems	½ hour
Review	Quantitative Comparisons	½ hour
½ hour break		
Review	Reading Comp.	½ hour
Review	Algebra	½ hour
Friday		
Review	Synonyms	½ hour
Review	Word Problems	½ hour
Review	Quantitative Comparisons	½ hour
½ hour break		
Review	Algebra	½ hour
Review	Reading Comp.	½ hour

Using this example, adapt the study plan to your own schedule. This schedule assumes 2 ½ - 3 hours available to study everyday for a 5 day period.

First, write out what you need to study and how much. Next figure out how many days you have before the test. Note, do NOT study on the last day before the test. On the last day before the test, you won't learn anything and will probably only confuse yourself.

Make a table with the days before the test and the number of hours you have available to study each day. We suggest working with 1 hour and ½ hour time slots.

Start filling in the blanks, with the subjects you need to study the most getting the most time and the most regular time slots (i.e. everyday) and the subjects that you know getting the least time (e.g. ½ hour every other day, or every 3rd day).

Tips for making a schedule

Once you make a schedule, stick with it! Make your study sessions reasonable. If you make a study schedule and don't stick with it, you set yourself up for failure. Instead, schedule study sessions that are a bit shorter and set yourself up for success! Make sure your study sessions are do-able. Studying is hard work but after you pass, you can party and take a break!

Schedule breaks. Breaks are just as important as study time. Work out a rotation of studying and breaks that works for you.

Build up study time. If you find it hard to sit still and study for 1 hour straight through, build up to it. Start with 20 minutes, and then take a break. Once you get used to 20-minute study sessions, increase the time to 30 minutes. Gradually work you way up to 1 hour.

40 minutes to 1 hour is optimal. Studying for longer than this is tiring and not productive. Studying for shorter isn't long enough to be productive.
Studying Math. Studying Math is different from studying other subjects because you use a different part of your brain. The best way to study math is to practice everyday. This will train your mind to think in a mathematical way. If you miss a day or days, the mathematical mind-set is gone, and you have to start all over again to build it up.

Study and practice math everyday for at least 5 days before the exam.

More Info on Making a Study Plan

How to study math

https://www.test-preparation.ca/study-math/

How to Study
For more information, see our How to Study Guide at
https://www.test-preparation.ca/learning-study/

Flash Cards - The Complete Guide

https://www.test-preparation.ca/flash-cards/

Using your Daily Routine to Study

https://www.test-preparation.ca/daily-routine/

Verbal Reasoning

This section contains a self-assessment and verbal reasoning tutorial. The tutorials are designed to familiarize general principles and the self-assessment contains general questions similar to the verbal reasoning questions likely to be on the ISEE®, but are not intended to be identical to the exam questions. The tutorials are not designed to be a complete reading course, and it is assumed that students have some familiarity with verbal reasoning questions. If you do not understand parts of the tutorial, or find the tutorial difficult, it is recommended that you seek out additional instruction.

Tour of the ISEE Verbal Reasoning

The ISEE® verbal reasoning section has 40 questions. Below is a more detailed list of the types of reading questions that generally appear on the ISEE®. Make sure you understand all these points at a very minimum.

- Synonyms
- Sentence Completion

The questions below are not the same as you will find on the ISEE® - that would be too easy! And nobody knows what the questions will be and they change all the time. Mostly the changes consist of substituting new questions for old, but the changes can be new question formats or styles, changes to the number of questions in each section, changes to the time limits for each section and combining sections. Below are general Verbal Reasoning questions that cover the same areas as the ISEE®. So, while the format and exact wording of the questions may differ slightly, and change from year to year, if you can answer the questions below, you will have no problem with the verbal reasoning section of the ISEE®.

Verbal Reasoning Self-Assessment

The purpose of the self-assessment is:

- Identify your strengths and weaknesses.
- Develop your personalized study plan (above)
- Get accustomed to the ISEE® format
- Extra practice – the self-assessments are almost a full 3rd practice test!
- Provide a baseline score for preparing your study schedule.

Since this is a Self-assessment, and depending on how confident you are with Verbal Reasoning, timing is optional. The ISEE® has 40 Verbal Reasoning questions to be answered in 20 minutes. The self-assessment has 30 questions, so allow about 10 minutes to complete this assessment.

Once complete, use the table below to assess your understanding of the content, and prepare your study schedule described in chapter 1.

80% - 100%	Excellent – you have mastered the content
60 – 79%	Good. You have a working knowledge. Even though you can just pass this section, you may want to review the tutorials and do some extra practice to see if you can improve your mark.
40% - 59%	Below Average. You do not understand verbal reasoning problems. Review the tutorials, and retake this quiz again in a few days, before proceeding to the practice test questions.
Less than 40%	Poor. You have a very limited understanding of verbal reasoning problems. Please review the tutorials, and retake this quiz again in a few days, before proceeding to the practice test questions.

Verbal Reasoning Self-Assessment Answer Sheet

1. A B C D
2. A B C D
3. A B C D
4. A B C D
5. A B C D
6. A B C D
7. A B C D
8. A B C D
9. A B C D
10. A B C D
11. A B C D
12. A B C D
13. A B C D
14. A B C D
15. A B C D
16. A B C D
17. A B C D
18. A B C D
19. A B C D
20. A B C D
21. A B C D
22. A B C D
23. A B C D
24. A B C D
25. A B C D
26. A B C D
27. A B C D
28. A B C D
29. A B C D
30. A B C D

Part I – Synonyms

Directions: Choose the word that is closest in meaning to the given word.

1. CONSPICUOUS

    a. Important
    b. Prominent
    c. Beautiful
    d. Convincing

2. BENEVOLENCE

    a. Happiness
    b. Courage
    c. Kindness
    d. Loyalty

3. BOISTEROUS

    a. Loud
    b. Soft
    c. Gentle
    d. Warm

4. FONDLE

    a. Hold
    b. Caress
    c. Throw
    d. Keep

5. MOMENTOUS

    a. Magical
    b. Memorable
    c. Extraordinary
    d. Very important

6. ANTAGONIST

    a. Supporter
    b. Fan
    c. Enemy
    d. Partner

7. MEMENTO

    a. Monument
    b. Remember
    c. Reminder
    d. Idea

8. INSIDIOUS

    a. Wise
    b. Brave
    c. Helpful
    d. Deceitful

9. ITINERARY

    a. Schedule
    b. Guidebook
    c. Pass
    d. Diary

10. ILLUSTRIOUS

    a. Rich
    b. Noble
    c. Gallant
    d. Poor

11. SUCCULENT

    a. Dull
    b. Adventurous
    c. Sweet
    d. Juicy

12. CONSTRUE

　a. Decide
　b. Design
　c. Interpret
　d. Examine

13. GREGARIOUS

　a. Sad
　b. Sociable
　c. Loving
　d. Funny

14. HESITANT

　a. Willing
　b. Doubtful
　c. Eager
　d. Happy

15. LUCID

　a. Dark
　b. Clear
　c. Memorable
　d. Easy

Part II - Sentence Completion

Directions: For each sentence below, choose the word that best completes the sentence.

16. When Joe broke his _____ in a skiing accident, his entire leg was in a cast.

　a. Ankle
　b. Humerus
　c. Wrist
　d. Femur

17. Alan had to learn the _____ system of numbering when his family moved to Great Britain.

　a. American
　b. Decimal
　c. Metric
　d. Fingers and toes

18. After Lisa's aunt had her tenth child, Lisa found that she had more than twenty _____ .

　a. Uncles
　b. Friends
　c. Stepsisters
　d. Cousins

19. Although he had flown many times, this was his first flight in a _____ .

　a. Helicopter
　b. Kite
　c. Train
　d. Subway car

20. George is very serious about his _____, and recently joined the American Scholastic Association.

　a. Schoolwork
　b. Cooking
　c. Travelling
　d. Athletics

21. She was a rabid Red Sox fan, attending every game, and demonstrating her _____ by cheering more loudly than anyone else.

    a. Knowledge
    b. Boredom
    c. Commitment
    d. Enthusiasm

22. When Craig's dog was struck by a car, he rushed his pet to the _____.

    a. Emergency room
    b. Doctor
    c. Veterinarian
    d. Podiatrist

23. After she received her influenza vaccination, Nan thought that she was _____ to the common cold.

    a. Immune
    b. Susceptible
    c. Vulnerable
    d. At risk

24. Paul's rose bushes were being destroyed by Japanese beetles, so he invested in a good _____.

    a. Fungicide
    b. Fertilizer
    c. Sprinkler
    d. Pesticide

25. The last time that the crops failed, the entire nation experienced months of _____.

    a. Famine
    b. Harvest
    c. Plenitude
    d. Disease

26. Because of a pituitary dysfunction, Karl lacked the necessary _____ to grow as tall as his father.

    a. Glands
    b. Hormones
    c. Vitamins
    d. Testosterone

27. Because of its colorful fall _____, the maple is my favorite tree.

    a. Growth
    b. Branches
    c. Greenery
    d. Foliage

28. When Mr. Davis returned from southern Asia, he told us about the _____ that sometimes swept the area, bringing torrential rain.

    a. Monsoons
    b. Hurricanes
    c. Blizzards
    d. Floods

29. Is it true that _____ always grows on the north side of trees?

    a. Lichens
    b. Moss
    c. Ferns
    d. Ground cover

30. You can _____ some fires by covering them with dirt, while others require foam or water.

    a. Extinguish
    b. Distinguish
    c. Ignite
    d. Lessen

Answer Key

Part I – Synonyms

1. B
Conspicuous and prominent are synonyms.

2. C
Benevolence and Kindness are synonyms.

3. A
Boisterous and loud are synonyms.

4. B
Fondle and caress are synonyms.

5. D
Momentous and very important are synonyms.

6. C
Antagonist and enemy are synonyms.

7. C
Memento and reminder are synonyms.

A memento is an object kept as a reminder or souvenir of a person or event.

8. D
Insidious and deceitful are synonyms.

Insidious means treacherous or crafty.

9. A
Itinerary and schedule are synonyms.

Itinerary is a travel document recording a trip or journey.

10. B
Illustrious and noble are synonyms.

Illustrious means well known, respected, and admired for past achievements.

11. D
Succulent and juicy are synonyms.

Succulent means tender, juicy, and tasty.

12. C
Construe and interpret are synonyms.

To construe means to interpret (a word or action) in a particular way.

13. B
Gregarious and sociable are synonyms.

Gregarious means fond of company; sociable.

14. B
Hesitant and doubtful are synonyms.

Hesitant means, tentative, unsure, or slow in acting or speaking.

15. B
Lucid and clear are synonyms.

Lucid means expressed clearly; easy to understand.

Part II – Sentence Completion

16. D
Femur NOUN A thighbone.

17. C
Metric System a system of measurements that is based on the base units of the meter/metre, the kilogram, the second, the ampere, the kelvin, the mole, and the candela.

18. D
Cousins NOUN the son or daughter of a person's uncle or aunt; a first cousin.

19. A
Helicopter

20. B
Schoolwork

21. D
Enthusiasm NOUN intensity of feeling; excited interest or eagerness.

22. C
Veterinarian NOUN medical doctor who treats non-human animals.

23. A
Immune ADJECTIVE protected by inoculation, or due to innate resistance to pathogens.

24. D
Pesticide NOUN a substance, usually synthetic although sometimes biological, used to kill or contain the activities of pests.

25. A
Famine NOUN a period of extreme shortage of food in a region.

26. B
Hormones NOUN any substance produced by one tissue and conveyed by the bloodstream to another to effect physiological activity.

27. D
Foliage NOUN the leaves of plants.

28. A
Monsoons NOUN tropical rainy season when the rain lasts for several months with few interruptions.

29. B
Moss NOUN any of various small green plants growing on the ground or on the surfaces of trees, stones etc.

30. A
Extinguish NOUN to put out, as in fire; to end burning; to quench.

QUANTITATIVE REASONING

THIS SECTION CONTAINS A SELF-ASSESSMENT AND QUANTITATIVE REASONING TUTORIAL. The tutorials are designed to familiarize general principles and the self-assessment contains general questions similar to the quantitative reasoning questions likely to be on the ISEE®, but are not intended to be identical to the exam questions. The tutorials are not designed to be a complete reading course, and it is assumed that students have some familiarity with quantitative reasoning questions. If you do not understand parts of the tutorial, or find the tutorial difficult, it is recommended that you seek out additional instruction.

Tour of the ISEE Quantitative Reasoning

The ISEE® Quantitative Reasoning section has 35 questions. Below is a detailed list of the types of reading questions that generally appear on the ISEE®. Make sure you understand all of these points at a very minimum.

- Problem Solving
- Quantitative Comparisons
- Word Problems
- Basic Math

The questions below are not the same as you will find on the ISEE® - that would be too easy! And nobody knows what the questions will be and they change all the time. Mostly the changes consist of substituting new questions for old, but the changes can be new question formats or styles, changes to the number of questions in each section, changes to the time limits for each section and combining sections. Below are general quantitative reasoning questions that cover the same areas as the ISEE®. So, while the format and exact wording of the questions may differ slightly, and change from year to year, if you can answer the questions below, you will have no problem with the quantitative reasoning section of the ISEE®.

Quantitative Reasoning Self-Assessment

The purpose of the self-assessment is:

- Identify your strengths and weaknesses.
- Develop your personalized study plan (above)
- Get accustomed to the ISEE® format
- Extra practice – the self-assessments are almost a full 3rd practice test!
- Provide a baseline score for preparing your study schedule.

Since this is a self-assessment, and depending on how confident you are with quantitative reasoning, timing is optional. The ISEE® has 35 Quantitative Reasoning questions to be answered in 35 minutes. The self-assessment has 25 questions, so allow about 25 minutes to complete this assessment.

Once complete, use the table below to assess your understanding of the content, and prepare your study schedule described in chapter 1.

80% - 100%	Excellent – you have mastered the content
60 – 79%	Good. You have a working knowledge. Even though you can just pass this section, you may want to review the tutorials and do some extra practice to see if you can improve your mark.
40% - 59%	Below Average. You do not understand quantitative reasoning problems. Review the tutorials, and retake this quiz again in a few days, before proceeding to the practice test questions.
Less than 40%	Poor. You have a very limited understanding of quantitative reasoning problems. Please review the tutorials, and retake this quiz again in a few days, before proceeding to the practice test questions.

Quantitative Reasoning Self-Assessment

1. Ⓐ Ⓑ Ⓒ Ⓓ   11. Ⓐ Ⓑ Ⓒ Ⓓ   21. Ⓐ Ⓑ Ⓒ Ⓓ
2. Ⓐ Ⓑ Ⓒ Ⓓ   12. Ⓐ Ⓑ Ⓒ Ⓓ   22. Ⓐ Ⓑ Ⓒ Ⓓ
3. Ⓐ Ⓑ Ⓒ Ⓓ   13. Ⓐ Ⓑ Ⓒ Ⓓ   23. Ⓐ Ⓑ Ⓒ Ⓓ
4. Ⓐ Ⓑ Ⓒ Ⓓ   14. Ⓐ Ⓑ Ⓒ Ⓓ   24. Ⓐ Ⓑ Ⓒ Ⓓ
5. Ⓐ Ⓑ Ⓒ Ⓓ   15. Ⓐ Ⓑ Ⓒ Ⓓ   25. Ⓐ Ⓑ Ⓒ Ⓓ
6. Ⓐ Ⓑ Ⓒ Ⓓ   16. Ⓐ Ⓑ Ⓒ Ⓓ
7. Ⓐ Ⓑ Ⓒ Ⓓ   17. Ⓐ Ⓑ Ⓒ Ⓓ
8. Ⓐ Ⓑ Ⓒ Ⓓ   18. Ⓐ Ⓑ Ⓒ Ⓓ
9. Ⓐ Ⓑ Ⓒ Ⓓ   19. Ⓐ Ⓑ Ⓒ Ⓓ
10. Ⓐ Ⓑ Ⓒ Ⓓ   20. Ⓐ Ⓑ Ⓒ Ⓓ

1. **What is 6 more than 1/3 of 25?**

    a. 8.33
    b. 15
    c. 14.33
    d. 18

2. **What number is the largest?**

    a. 50% of 50
    b. 2/5 of 200
    c. 0.2 portion of 20
    d. 1/5th of 30

3. **15 is what percent of 200?**

    a. 30%
    b. 15%
    c. 20%
    d. 7.50%

4. **A boy has 5 red balls, 3 white balls and 2 yellow balls. What percent of the balls are yellow?**

    a. 2%
    b. 8%
    c. 20%
    d. 12%

5. **Convert 0.45 to a fraction**

    a. 7/20
    b. 7/45
    c. 9/20
    d. 3/20

6. **What is 1/3 of 3/4?**

    a. 1/4
    b. 1/3
    c. 2/3
    d. 3/4

7. **What fraction of $1500 is $75?**

    a. 1/14
    b. 3/5
    c. 7/10
    d. 1/12

8. **What is 2/4 X 3/4 reduced to lowest terms?**

    a. 6/12
    b. 3/8
    c. 6/16
    d. 3/4

9. **How many grams is 10 kg?**

    a. 10,000 grams
    b. 1,000 grams
    c. 100 grams
    d. 10.11 grams

10. **A man buys an item for $420 and has a balance of $3000.00. How much did he have before?**

    a. $2,580
    b. $3,420
    c. $2,420
    d. $342

11. **Divide 0.123 by 10^3**

    a. 1.23
    b. 0.0123
    c. 0.00123
    d. 0.000123

12. $x^{-5}/x^{-3} \times x^5/x^3$

   a. -1
   b. 0
   c. 1
   d. X^{-1}

Part II

Directions: Examine the quantities given in Column A and Column B of the table and choose the best answer.

13.

Column A	Column B
5x	4x + 2

$7x - 9 = 47$

   a. Column A is greater
   b. Column B is greater
   c. The quantities are equal
   d. The relationship cannot be determined

14.

Column A	Column B
The average of the set below	10.5

{5, 9, 12, 15}

   a. Column A is greater
   b. Column B is greater
   c. The quantities are equal
   d. The relationship cannot be determined

15.

Column A	Column B
25% of 60	19% of 45

   a. Column A is greater
   b. Column B is greater
   c. The quantities are equal
   d. The relationship cannot be determined

16.

Column A	Column B
2,199 + 5,832 =	3,406 - 2,767 =

   a. Column A is greater
   b. Column B is greater
   c. The quantities are equal
   d. The relationship cannot be determined

17.

Column A	Column B
6.75 / 3.2	4.2 / 1.4

   a. Column A is greater
   b. Column B is greater
   c. The quantities are equal
   d. The relationship cannot be determined

18.

Column A	Column B
2Y + 3	3Y - 5

$7(2y + 8) = 168$

   a. Column A is greater
   b. Column B is greater
   c. The quantities are equal
   d. The relationship cannot be determined

19.

Column A	Column B
2/5 + 3/4	6/9 + 5/6

   a. Column A is greater
   b. Column B is greater
   c. The quantities are equal
   d. The relationship cannot be determined

20.

Column A	Column B
Bill's Savings	$80

Bill bought a dishwasher for 25% off. The retail price was $300.

   a. Column A is greater
   b. Column B is greater
   c. The quantities are equal
   d. The relationship cannot be determined

21.

Column A	Column B
x^2	x + 3

x <= 2

   a. Column A is greater
   b. Column B is greater
   c. The quantities are equal
   d. The relationship cannot be determined

22.

Column A	Column B
35% of 135	25% of 150

   a. Column A is greater
   b. Column B is greater
   c. The quantities are equal
   d. The relationship cannot be determined

23.

Column A	Column B
8.7 – 4.3	5.2 + 3.1

   a. Column A is greater
   b. Column B is greater
   c. The quantities are equal
   d. The relationship cannot be determined

24.

Column A	Column B
6.73 X 8	7.2 X 4.7

   a. Column A is greater
   b. Column B is greater
   c. The quantities are equal
   d. The relationship cannot be determined

25.

Column A	Column B
Z	15

3Z + 12 = 60

   a. Column A is greater
   b. Column B is greater
   c. The quantities are equal
   d. The relationship cannot be determined

Answer Key

1. C
1/3 of 25 = 8.33 + 6 = 14.33

2. B

 a. 50% of 50 = 25
 b. 2/5 of 200 = 80
 c. 0.2 portion of 20 = 4
 d. 1/5 of 30 = 6

B is the largest.

3. A
15% = 15/100 X 200 = 7.5%

4. C
Total number of balls = 10, number of yellow balls = 2. So 2/10 X 100 = 20%

5. C
0.45 = 45/100 = 9/20

6. A
1/3 X 3/4 = 3/12 = 1/4

7. D
75/1500 = 15/300 = 3/60 = 1/12

8. B
2/4 X 3/4 = 6/16, and lowest terms = 3/8

9. A
1kg = 1,000 g and 10 kg = 10 x 1,000 = 10,000 g

10. B
(Amount Spent) $420 + $3000 (Balance) = $3420

11. D
$0.123 / 10^3$ = 0.000123

12. C
x^{-5}/x^{-3} X x^5/x^3 = 1

13. A
7x – 9 = 47
X = 8
So 5X > 4X + 2

14. B
The average = (5 + 9 + 12 + 15)/4 = 10.25 < 10.5

15. A
25% of 60 = 15
19% of 45 = 8.55

16. A
2,199 + 5,832 = 8.031
3,406 - 2,767 = 639

17. B
6.75 / 3.2 = 2.109
4.2 / 1.4 = 3

18. C
7(2y + 8) = 168
Y = 8
2Y + 3 = 19
3Y -5 = 19

19. B
2/5 + ¾ = 4/20 + 15/20 = 19/20
6/9 + 5/6 = 24/36 + 30/36 = 54/36

20. A
25% X $300 = 75

21. B

22. A
35% of 135 = 47.25
25% of 150 = 37.50

23. B
8.7 – 4.3 = 4.4
5.2 + 3.1 = 8.3

24. B
6.73 X 8 = 53.84
7.2 X 4.7 = 33.84

25. A
3Z + 12 = 60
Z = 16

Reading Comprehension

This section contains a self-assessment and reading comprehension tutorial. The tutorials are designed to familiarize general principles and the self-assessment contains general questions similar to the reading questions likely to be on the ISEE®, but are not intended to be identical to the exam questions. The tutorials are not designed to be a complete reading course, and it is assumed that students have some familiarity with reading comprehension and vocabulary questions. If you do not understand parts of the tutorial, or find the tutorial difficult, it is recommended that you seek out additional instruction.

Tour of the ISEE Reading Comprehension Content

Below is more detailed list of the types of reading comprehension questions that generally appear on the ISEE®. Make sure you understand all of these points at a very minimum.

- Drawing logical conclusions
- Make predictions
- Analyze and evaluate the use of text structure to solve problems or identify sequences
- Vocabulary - Give the definition of a word from context
- Summarizing

The questions below are not the same as you will find on the ISEE® - that would be too easy! And nobody knows what the questions will be and they change all the time. Mostly the changes consist of substituting new questions for old, but the changes can be new question formats or styles, changes to the number of questions in each section, changes to the time limits for each section and combining sections. Below are general reading comprehension questions that cover the same areas as the ISEE®. So, while the format and exact wording of the questions may differ slightly, and change from year to year, if you can answer the questions below, you will have no problem with the reading comprehension section of the ISEE®.

Reading Self-Assessment

The purpose of the self-assessment is:

- Identify your strengths and weaknesses.
- Develop your personalized study plan (above)
- Get accustomed to the ISEE® format
- Extra practice – the self-assessments are almost a full 3rd practice test!
- Provide a baseline score for preparing your study schedule.

Since this is a self-assessment, and depending on how confident you are with reading comprehension and vocabulary, timing is optional. The ISEE® has 40 reading comprehension questions to be answered in 40 minutes. The self-assessment has 18 questions, so allow about 20 minutes to complete this assessment.

Once complete, use the table below to assess your understanding of the content, and prepare your study schedule described in chapter 1.

For more practice with reading comprehension, see our Multiple Choice secrets book at www.multiple-choice.ca.

80% - 100%	Excellent – you have mastered the content
60 – 79%	Good. You have a working knowledge. Even though you can just pass this section, you may want to review the tutorials and do some extra practice to see if you can improve your mark.
40% - 59%	Below Average. You do not understand reading comprehension problems. Review the tutorials , and retake this quiz again in a few days, before proceeding to the practice test questions.
Less than 40%	Poor. You have a very limited understanding of reading comprehension problems. Please review the tutorials , and retake this quiz again in a few days, before proceeding to the practice test questions.

Reading Self-Assessment Answer Sheet

1. A B C D
2. A B C D
3. A B C D
4. A B C D
5. A B C D
6. A B C D
7. A B C D
8. A B C D
9. A B C D
10. A B C D
11. A B C D
12. A B C D
13. A B C D
14. A B C D
15. A B C D
16. A B C D
17. A B C D
18. A B C D

Questions 1 – 4 refer to the following passage.

Passage 1 - The Immune System

An immune system is a system of biological structures and processes that protects against disease by identifying and killing pathogens and other threats. The immune system can detect a wide variety of agents, from viruses to parasitic worms, and distinguish them from the organism's own healthy cells and tissues. Detection is complicated as pathogens evolve rapidly to avoid the immune system defences, and successfully infect their hosts.

The human immune system consists of many types of proteins, cells, organs, and tissues, which interact in an elaborate and dynamic network. As part of this more complex immune response, the human immune system adapts over time to recognize specific pathogens more efficiently. This adaptation process is called "adaptive immunity" or "acquired immunity" and creates immunological memory. Immunological memory created from a primary response to a specific pathogen, provides an enhanced response to future encounters with that same pathogen. This process of acquired immunity is the basis of vaccination.

https://en.wikipedia.org/wiki/Immune_system.

1. What can we infer from the first paragraph in this passage?

   a. When a person's body fights off the flu, this is the immune system in action
   b. When a person's immune system functions correctly, they avoid all sicknesses and injuries
   c. When a person's immune system is weak, a person will likely get a terminal disease
   d. When a person's body fights off a cold, this is the circulatory system in action

2. The immune system's primary function is to:

   a. Strengthen the bones
   b. Protect against disease
   c. Improve respiration
   d. Improve circulation

3. Based on the passage, what can we say about evolution's role in the immune system?

a. Evolution of the immune system is an important factor in the immune system's efficiency

b. Evolution causes a person to die, thus killing the pathogen

c. Evolution plays no known role in immunity

d. The least evolved earth species have better immunity

4. Which sentence below, taken from the passage, tell us the main idea of the passage?

a. The human immune system consists of many types of proteins, cells, organs, and tissues, which interact in an elaborate and dynamic network.

b. An immune system is a system of biological structures and processes that protects against disease by identifying and killing pathogens and other threats.

c. The immune system can detect a wide variety of agents, from viruses to parasitic worms, and distinguish them from the organism's own healthy cells and tissues.

d. None of these express the main idea.

Questions 5 – 8 refer to the following passage.

Passage 2 - White Blood Cells

White blood cells (WBCs), or leukocytes (also spelled "leucocytes"), are cells of the immune system that defend the body against both infectious disease and foreign material. Five different and diverse types of leukocytes exist, but they are all produced and derived from a powerful cell in the bone marrow known as a hematopoietic stem cell. Leukocytes are found throughout the body, including the blood and lymphatic system.

The number of WBCs in the blood is often an indicator of disease. There are normally between 4×10^9 and 1.1×10^{10} white blood cells in a liter of blood, making up about 1% of blood in a healthy adult. The physical properties of white blood cells, such as volume, conductivity, and granularity, changes due to the presence of immature cells, or malignant cells.

The name white blood cell derives from the fact that after processing a blood sample in a centrifuge, the white cells are typically a thin, white layer of nucleated cells. The scientific term leukocyte directly reflects this description, derived from Greek leukos (white), and kytos (cell).

https://en.wikipedia.org/wiki/White_blood_cell.

5. What can we infer from the first paragraph in this selection?

    a. Red blood cells are not as important as white blood cells

    b. White blood cells are the culprits in most infectious diseases

    c. White blood cells are essential to fight off infectious diseases

    d. Red blood cells are essential to fight off infectious diseases

6. What can we say about the number of white blood cells in a liter of blood?

    a. They make up about 1% of a healthy adult's blood

    b. There are 10^{10} WBCs in a healthy adult's blood

    c. The number varies according to age

    d. They are a thin white layer of nucleated cells

7. What is a more scientific term for "white blood cell?"

    a. Red blood cell

    b. Anthrocyte

    c. Leukocyte

    d. Leukemia

8. Can the number of leukocytes indicate cancer?

    a. Yes, the white blood cell count can indicate disease.

    b. No, the white blood cell count is not a reliable indicator.

    c. Disease may indicate a high white blood cell count.

    d. None of the choices are correct.

Questions 9 – 12 refer to the following passage.

Keeping Tropical Fish

Keeping tropical fish at home or in your office used to be very popular. Today interest has declined, but it remains as rewarding and relaxing a hobby as ever. Ask any tropical fish hobbyist, and you will hear how soothing and relaxing watching colorful fish live their lives in the aquarium. If you are considering keeping tropical fish as pets, here is a list of the basic equipment you will need.

A filter is essential for keeping your aquarium clean and your fish alive and healthy. There are different types and sizes of filters and the right size for you depends on the size of the aquarium and the level of stocking. Generally, you need a filter with a 3 to 5 times turn over rate per hour. This means that the water in the tank should go through the filter about 3 to 5 times per hour.

Most tropical fish do well in water temperatures ranging between 24°C and 26°C, though each has its own ideal water temperature. A heater with a thermostat is necessary to regulate the water temperature. Some heaters are submersible and others are not, so check carefully before you buy.

Lights are also necessary, and come in a large variety of types, strengths and sizes. A light source is necessary for plants in the tank to photosynthesize and give the tank a more attractive appearance. Even if you plan to use plastic plants, the fish still require light, although here, you can use a lower strength light source.

A hood is necessary to keep dust, dirt and unwanted materials out of the tank. Sometimes the hood can also help prevent evaporation. Another requirement is aquarium gravel. This will improve the aesthetics of the aquarium and is necessary if you plan to have real plants.

9. What is the general tone of this article?

a. Formal
b. Informal
c. Technical
d. Opinion

10. Which of the following can not be inferred?

a. Gravel is good for aquarium plants.
b. Fewer people have aquariums in their office than at home.
c. The larger the tank, the larger the filter required.
d. None of the above.

11. What evidence does the author provide to support their claim that aquarium lights are necessary?

a. Plants require light.
b. Fish and plants require light.
c. The author does not provide evidence for this statement.
d. Aquarium lights make the aquarium more attractive.

12. Which of the following is an opinion?

a. Filter with a 3 to 5 times turn over rate per hour are required.
b. Aquarium gravel improves the aesthetics of the aquarium.
c. An aquarium hood keeps dust, dirt and unwanted materials out of the tank.
d. Each type of tropical fish has its own ideal water temperature.

Questions 13 – 14 refer to the following passage.

Vice President Johnson, Mr. Speaker, Mr. Chief Justice, President Eisenhower, Vice President Nixon, President Truman, reverend clergy, fellow citizens:

We observe today not a victory of party, but a celebration of freedom -- symbolizing an end, as well as a beginning -- signifying renewal, as well as change. For I have sworn before you and Almighty God the same solemn oath our forebears prescribed nearly a century and three-quarters ago.

The world is very different now. For man holds in his mortal hands the power to abolish all forms of human poverty and all forms of human life. And yet the same revolutionary beliefs for which our forebears fought are still at issue around the globe -- the belief that the rights of man come not from the generosity of the state, but from the hand of God.

We dare not forget today that we are the heirs of that first revolution. Let the word go forth from this time and place, to friend and foe alike, that the torch has been passed to a new generation of Americans -- born in this century, tempered by war, disciplined by a hard and bitter peace, proud of our ancient heritage, and unwilling to witness or permit the slow undoing of those human rights to which this nation has always been committed, and to which we are committed today at home and around the world.

Let every nation know, whether it wishes us well or ill, that we shall pay any price, bear any burden, meet any hardship, support any friend, oppose any foe, to assure the survival and the success of liberty.

This much we pledge -- and more.

John F. Kennedy Inaugural Address 20 January 1961

13. What is the tone of this speech?

a. Triumphant
b. Optimistic
c. Threatening
d. Gloating

14. Which of the following is an opinion?

a. The world is very different now.
b. For man holds in his mortal hands the power to abolish all forms of human poverty and all forms of human life.
c. We dare not forget today that we are the heirs of that first revolution
d. For I have sworn before you and Almighty God the same solemn oath our forebears prescribed nearly a century and three-quarters ago.

Multiple Choice Strategy

Questions 15 – 18 refer to the following passage and test your skills at answering reading comprehension multiple choice questions strategically.

If You Have Allergies, You're Not Alone

People who experience allergies might joke that their immune systems have let them down or are seriously lacking. Truthfully though, people who experience allergic reactions or allergy symptoms during certain times of the year have heightened immune systems that are, "better" than those of people who have perfectly healthy but less militant immune systems.
Still, when a person has an allergic reaction, they are having an adverse reaction to a substance that is considered normal to most people. Mild allergic reactions usually have symptoms like itching, runny nose, red eyes, or bumps or discoloration of the skin. More serious allergic reactions, such as those to animal and insect poisons or certain foods, may result in the closing of the throat, swelling of the eyes, low blood pressure, an inability to breathe, and can even be fatal.

Different treatments help different allergies, and which one a person uses depends on the nature and severity of the allergy. It is recommended to patients with severe allergies to take extra precautions, such as carrying an EpiPen, which treats anaphylactic shock and may prevent death, always in order for the remedy to be readily available and more effective. When an allergy is not so severe, treatments may be used just relieve a person of uncomfortable symptoms. Over the counter allergy medicines treat milder symptoms, and can be bought at any grocery store and used in moderation to help people with allergies live normally.

There are many tests available to assess whether a person has allergies or what they may be allergic to, and advances in these tests and the medicine used to treat patients continues to improve. Despite this fact, allergies still affect many people throughout the year or even every day. Medicines used to treat allergies have side effects of their own, and it is difficult to bring the body into balance with the use of medicine. Regardless, many of those who live with allergies are grateful for what is available and find it useful in maintaining their lifestyles.

15. According to this passage, it can be understood that the word "militant" belongs in a group with the words:

    a. sickly, ailing, faint
    b. strength, power, vigor
    c. active, fighting, warring
    d. worn, tired, breaking down

16. The author says that "medicines used to treat allergies have side effects of their own" in order to

   a. point out that doctors aren't very good at diagnosing and treating allergies.

   b. argue that because of the large number of people with allergies, a cure will never be found.

   c. explain that allergy medicines aren't cures and some compromise must be made.

   d. argue that more wholesome remedies should be researched and medicines banned.

17. It can be inferred that _____ recommend that some people with allergies carry medicine with them.

   a. the author
   b. doctors
   c. the makers of EpiPen
   d. people with allergies

18. The author has written this passage in order to

   a. inform readers on symptoms of allergies so people with allergies can get help.

   b. persuade readers to be proud of having allergies.

   c. inform readers on different remedies so people with allergies receive the right help.

   d. describe different types of allergies, their symptoms, and their remedies.

Answer Key

1. A
The passage does not mention the flu specifically, however we know the flu is a pathogen (a bacterium, virus, or other microorganism that can cause disease). Therefore, we can infer, when a person's body fights off the flu, this is the immune system in action.

2. B
The immune system's primary function is to protect against disease.

3. A
The passage refers to evolution of the immune system being important for efficiency. In paragraph three, there is a discussion of adaptive and acquired immunity, where the immune system "remembers" pathogens.

We can conclude, evolution of the immune system is an important factor in the immune system's efficiency.

4. B
The sentence that expresses the main idea of the passage is, "An immune system is a system of biological structures and processes that protects against disease by identifying and killing pathogens and other threats."

5. C
We can infer white blood cells are essential to fight off infectious diseases, from the passage, "cells of the immune system that defend the body against both infectious disease and foreign material."

6. A
We can say the quantity of white blood cells in a liter of blood make up about 1% of a healthy adult's blood. This is a fact-based question that is easy and fast to answer. The question asks about a percentage. You can quickly and easily scan the passage for the percent sign, or the word percent and find the answer.

7. C
A more scientific term for "white blood cell" is leukocyte, from the first paragraph, first sentence of the passage.

8. A
The white blood cell count can indicate disease (cancer). We know this from the last sentence of paragraph two, "The physical properties of white blood cells, such as volume, conductivity, and granularity, changes due to the presence of immature cells, or malignant cells."

9. B
The general tone is informal.

10. B
The statement, "Fewer people have aquariums in their office than at home," cannot be inferred from this article.

11. C
The author does not provide evidence for this statement.

12. B
The following statement is an opinion, " Aquarium gravel improves the aesthetics of the aquarium."

13. A
This is a triumphant speech where President Kennedy is celebrating his victory.

14. C
The statement, "We dare not forget today that we are the heirs of that first revolution" is an opinion.

Multiple Choice Strategy

15. C
This question tests the reader's vocabulary skills. The uses of the negatives "but" and "less," especially right next to each other, may confuse readers into answering with choices A or D, which list words that are antonyms of "militant." Readers may also be confused by the comparison of healthy people with what is being described as an overly healthy person--both people are good, but the reader may look for which one is "worse" in the comparison, and therefore stray toward the antonyms. One key to understanding the meaning of "militant" if the reader is unfamiliar with it, is to look at the root of the word; readers can then easily associate it with "military" and gain a sense of what the word signifies: defense (especially considered that the immune system defends the body). Choice C is correct over B because "militant" is an adjective, just as the words in choice C are, whereas the words in choice B are nouns.

16. C
This question tests the reader's understanding of function within writing. The other choices are all details included surrounding the quoted text, and may therefore confuse the reader. Choice A somewhat contradicts what is said earlier in the paragraph, which is that tests and treatments are improving, and probably doctors are along with them, but the paragraph doesn't actually mention doctors, and the subject of the question is the medicine. Choice B may seem correct if you aren't careful to understand that, while the author does mention the large number of people affected, the author is touching on the realities of living with allergies rather than about the likelihood of curing all allergies. Similarly, while the author does mention the "balance" of the body, which is easily associated with "wholesome," the author is not really making an argument and especially is not making an extreme statement that allergy medicines should be outlawed. Again, because the article's tone is on living with allergies, choice C is an appropriate choice that fits with the title and content of the text.

17. B
This question tests the reader's inference skills. The text does not state who is doing the recommending, but the use of the "patients," as well as the general context of the passage, lends itself to the logical partner, "doctors," choice B. The author does mention the recommendation but doesn't present it as her own (i.e. "I recommend that"), so choice A may be eliminated. It may seem plausible that people with allergies (D) may recommend medicines or products to other people with allergies, but the text does not necessarily support this interaction taking place. Choice C may be selected because the EpiPen is specifically mentioned, but the use of the phrase "such as" when it is introduced is not limiting enough to assume the recommendation is coming from its creators.

18. D
This question tests the reader's global understanding of the text. Choice D includes the main topics of the three body paragraphs, and isn't too focused on a specific aspect or quote from the text, as the other questions are, giving a skewed summary of what the author intended. The reader may be drawn to choice B because of the title of the passage and the use of words like "better," but the message of the passage is larger and more general than this.

Help with Reading Comprehension

At first sight, reading comprehension tests look challenging especially if you are given long essays to answer only two to three questions. While reading, you might notice your attention wandering, or you may feel sleepy. Do not be discouraged because there are various tactics and long range strategies that make comprehending even long, boring essays easier.

Your friends before your foes. It is always best to tackle essays or passages with familiar subjects rather than those with unfamiliar ones. This approach applies the same logic as tackling easy questions before hard ones. Skip passages that do not interest you and leave them for later when there is more time left.

Don't use 'special' reading techniques. This is not the time for speed-reading or anything like that – just plain ordinary reading – not too slow and not too fast.

Read through the entire passage and the questions before you do anything. Many students try reading the questions first and then looking for answers in the passage thinking this approach is more efficient. What these students do not realize is that it is often hard to navigate in unfamiliar roads. If you do not familiarize yourself with the passage first, looking for answers become not only time-consuming but also dangerous because you might miss the context of the answer you are looking for. If you read the questions first you will only confuse yourself and lose valuable time.

Familiarize yourself with reading comprehension questions. If you are familiar with the common types of reading questions, you are able to take note of important parts of the passage, saving time. There are six major kinds of reading questions.

- **Main Idea**- Questions that ask for the central thought or significance of the passage.

- **Specific Details** - Questions that asks for explicitly stated ideas.

- **Drawing Inferences** - Questions that ask for a statement's intended meaning.

- **Tone or Attitude** - Questions that test your ability to sense the emotional state of the author.

- **Context Meaning** – Questions that ask for the meaning of a word depending on the context.

- **Technique** – Questions that ask for the method of organization or the writing style of the author.

Read. Read. Read. The best preparation for reading comprehension tests is always to read, read and read. If you are not used to reading lengthy passages, you will probably lose concentration. Increase your attention span by making a habit out of reading.

Reading comprehension tests become less daunting when you have trained yourself to read and understand fast. Always remember that it is easier to understand passages you are interested in. Do not read through passages hastily. Make mental notes of ideas that you think might be asked.

Reading Strategy

When facing the reading comprehension section of a standardized test, you need a strategy to be successful. You want to keep several steps in mind:

- **First, make a note of the time and the number of sections**. Time your work accordingly. Typically, four to five minutes per section is sufficient. Second, read the directions for each selection thoroughly before beginning (and listen well to any additional verbal instructions, as they will often clarify obscure or confusing written guidelines). You must know exactly how to do what you're about to do!

- **Now you're ready to begin reading the selection**. Read the passage carefully, noting significant characters or events on a scratch sheet of paper or underlining on the test sheet. Many students find making a basic list in the margins helpful. Quickly jot down or underline one-word summaries of characters, notable happenings, numbers, or key ideas. This will help you better retain information and focus wandering thoughts. Remember, however, that your main goal in doing this is to find the information that answers the questions. Even if you find the passage interesting, remember your goal and work fast but stay on track.

- Now read the question and all the choices. Now you have read the passage, have a general idea of the main ideas, and have marked the important points. Read the question and all the choices. Never choose an answer without reading them all! Questions are often designed to confuse – stay focussed and clear. Usually the answer choices will focus on one or two facts or inferences from the passage. Keep these clear in your mind.

- **Search for the answer**. With a very general idea of what the different choices are, go back to the passage and scan for the relevant information. Watch for big words, unusual or unique words. These make your job easier as you can scan the text for the particular word.

- Mark the Answer. Now you have the key information the question is looking for. Go back to the question, quickly scan the choices and mark the correct one.

Understand and practice the different types of standardized reading comprehension tests. See the list above for the different types. Typically, there will be several questions dealing with facts from the selection, a couple more inference questions dealing with logical consequences of those facts, and periodically an application-oriented question surfaces to force you to make connections with what you already know. Some students prefer to answer the questions as listed, and feel classifying the question and then ordering is wasting precious time. Other students prefer to answer the different types of questions in order of how easy or difficult they are. The choice is yours and do whatever works for you. If you want to try answering in order of difficulty, here is a recommended order, answer fact questions first; they're easily found within the passage. Tackle inference problems next, after re-reading the question(s) as many times as you need to. Application or 'best guess' questions usually take the longest, so save them for last.

Use the practice tests to try out both ways of answering and see what works for you.

For more help with reading comprehension, see Multiple Choice Secrets.

Main Idea and Supporting Details

Identifying the main idea, topic and supporting details in a passage can feel like an overwhelming task. The passages used for standardized tests can be boring and seem difficult - Test writers don't use interesting passages or ones that talk about things most people are familiar with. Despite these obstacles, all passages and paragraphs will have the information you need to answer the questions.

The topic of a passage or paragraph is its subject. It's the general idea and can be summed up in a word or short phrase. On some standardized tests, there is a short description of the passage if it's taken from a longer work. Make sure you read the description as it might state the topic of the passage. If not, read the passage and ask yourself, "Who or what is this about?" For example:

> Over the years, school uniforms have been hotly debated. Arguments are made that students have the right to show individuality and express themselves by choosing their own clothes. However, this brings up social and academic issues. Some kids cannot afford to wear the clothes they like and might be bullied by the "better dressed" students. With attention drawn to clothes and the individual, students will lose focus on class work and the reason they are in school. School uniforms should be mandatory.

Ask: What is this paragraph about?

Topic: school uniforms

Once you have the topic, it's easier to find the main idea. The main idea is a specific statement telling what the writer wants you to know about the topic. Writers usually state the main idea as a thesis statement. If you're looking for the main idea of a single paragraph, the main idea is called the topic sentence and will probably be the first or last sentence. If you're looking for the main idea of an entire passage, look for the thesis statement in either the first or last paragraph. The main idea is usually restated in the conclusion. To find the main idea of a passage or paragraph, follow these steps:

    1. Find the topic.

    2. Ask yourself, "What point is the author trying to make about the topic?"

    3. Create your own sentence summarizing the author's point.

    4. Look in the text for the sentence closest in meaning to yours.

Look at the example paragraph again. It's already established that the topic of the paragraph is school uniforms. What is the main idea/topic sentence?

Ask: "What point is the author trying to make about school uniforms?"

Summary: Students should wear school uniforms.

Topic sentence: School uniforms should be mandatory.

Main Idea: School uniforms should be mandatory.

Each paragraph offers supporting details to explain the main idea. The details could be facts or reasons, but they will always answer a question about the main idea. What? Where? Why? When? How? How much/many? Look at the example paragraph again. You'll notice that more than one sentence answers a question about the main idea. These are the supporting details.

Main Idea: School uniforms should be mandatory.

Ask: Why? Some kids cannot afford to wear clothes they like and could be bullied by the "better dressed" kids. Supporting Detail

With attention drawn to clothes and the individual, Students will lose focus on class work and the reason they are in school. Supporting Detail

What if the author doesn't state the main idea in a topic sentence? The passage will have an implied main idea. It's not as difficult to find as it might seem. Paragraphs are always organized around ideas. To find an implied main idea, you need to know the topic and then find the relationship between the supporting details. Ask yourself, "What is the point the author is making about the relationship between the details?."

Cocoa is what makes chocolate good for you. Chocolate comes in many varieties. These delectable flavors include milk chocolate, dark chocolate, semi-sweet, and white chocolate.

Ask: What is this paragraph about?

Topic: Chocolate

Ask: What? Where? Why? When? How? How much/many?

Supporting details: Chocolate is good for you because it is made of cocoa, Chocolate is delicious, Chocolate comes in different delicious flavors

Ask: What is the relationship between the details and what is the author's point?

Main Idea: Chocolate is good because it is healthy and it tastes good.

Testing Tips for Main Idea Questions

1. Skim the questions – not the answer choices - before reading the passage.

2. Questions about main idea might use the words "theme," "generalization," or "purpose."

3. Save questions about the main idea for last. On standardized tests like the SAT, the answers to the rest of the questions can be found in order in the passage.

3. Underline topic sentences in the passage. Most tests allow you to write in your testing booklet.

4. Answer the question in your own words before looking at the answer choices. Then match your answer with an answer choice.

5. Cross out incorrect answer choices immediately to prevent confusion.

6. If two of the answer choices mean the same thing but use different words, they are BOTH incorrect.

7. If a question asks about the whole passage, cross out the answer choices that apply only to part of it.

8. If only part of the information is correct, that answer choice is incorrect.

9. An answer choice that is too broad is incorrect. All information needs to be backed up by the passage.

10. Answer choices with extreme wording are usually incorrect.

Drawing Inferences And Conclusions

Drawing inferences and making conclusions happens all the time. In fact, you probably do it every time you read—sometimes without even realizing it! For example, remember the first time you saw the movie "The Lion King." When you meet Scar for the first time, he is trapping a helpless mouse with his sharp claws preparing to eat it. When you see this action you guess that Scar is going to be a bad character in the movie. Nothing appeared to tell you this. No caption came across the bottom of the screen that said "Bad Guy." No red arrow pointed to Scar and said "Evil Lion." No, you made an inference about his character based on the context clue you were given. You do the same thing when you read!

When you draw an inference or make a conclusion you are doing the same thing, you are making an educated guess based on the hints the author gives you. We call these hints "context clues." Scar trapping the innocent mouse is the context clue about Scar's character.

Usually you are making inferences and drawing conclusions the entire time that you are reading. Whether you realize it or not, you are constantly making educated guesses based on context clues. Think about a time you were reading a book and something happened that you were expecting to happen. You're not psychic! Actually, you were picking up on the context clues and making inferences about what was going to happen next!

Let's try an easy example. Read the following sentences and answer the questions at the end of the passage.

Shelly really likes to help people. She loves her job because she gets to help people every single day. However, Shelly has to work long hours and she can get called in the middle of the night for emergencies. She wears a white lab coat at work and usually she carries a stethoscope.

What is most likely Shelly's job?

    a. Musician
    b. Lawyer
    c. Doctor
    d. Teacher

This probably seemed easy. Drawing inferences isn't always this simple, but it is the same basic principle. How did you know Shelly was a doctor? She helps people, she works long hours, she wears a white lab coat, and she gets called in for emergencies at night. Context Clues! Nowhere in the paragraph did it say Shelly was a doctor, but you were able to draw that conclusion based on the information provided in the paragraph. This is how it's done!

There is a catch, though. Remember that when you draw inferences based on reading, you should only use the information given to you by the author. Sometimes it is easy for us to make conclusions based on knowledge that is already in our mind—but that can lead you to drawing an incorrect inference. For example, let's pretend there is a bully at your school named Brent. Now let's say you read a story and the main character's name is Brent. You could NOT infer that the character in the story is a bully just because his name is Brent. You should only use the information given to you by the author to avoid drawing the wrong conclusion.

Let's try another example. Read the passage below and answer the question.

Social media is an extremely popular new form of connecting and communicating over the internet. Since Facebook's original launch in 2004, millions of people have joined in the social media craze. In fact, it is estimated that almost 75% of all internet users aged 18 and older use some form of social media. Facebook started at Harvard University as a way to get students connected. However, it quickly grew into a worldwide phenomenon and today, the founder of Facebook, Mark Zuckerberg has an estimated net worth of 28.5 billion dollars.

Facebook is not the only social media platform, though. Other sites such as Twitter, Instagram, and Snapchat have since been invented and are quickly becoming just as popular! Many social media users actually use more than one type of social media. Furthermore, most social media sites have created mobile apps that allow people to connect via social media virtually anywhere in the world!

What is the most likely reason that other social media sites like Twitter and Instagram were created?

    a. Professors at Harvard University made it a class project.

    b. Facebook was extremely popular and other people thought they could also be successful by designing social media sites.

    c. Facebook was not connecting enough people.

    d. Mark Zuckerberg paid people to invent new social media sites because he wanted lots of competition.

Here, the correct answer is B. Facebook was extremely popular and other people thought they could also be successful by designing social media sites. How do we know this? What are the context clues? Take a look at the first paragraph. What do we know based on this paragraph? Well, one sentence refers to Facebook's original launch. This suggests that Facebook was one of the first social media sites. In addition, we know that the founder of Facebook has been extremely successful and is worth billions of dollars. From this we can infer that other people wanted to imitate Facebook's idea and become just as successful as Mark Zuckerberg.

Let's go through the other answers. If you chose A, it might be because Facebook started at Harvard University, so you drew the conclusion that all other social media sites were also started at Harvard University. However, there is no mention of class projects, professors, or students designing social media. So there doesn't seem to be enough support for choice A.

If you chose C, you might have been drawing your own conclusions based on outside information. Maybe none of your friends are on Facebook, so you made an inference that Facebook didn't connect enough people, so more sites were invented. Or maybe you think the people who connect on Facebook are too old, so you don't think Facebook connects enough people your age. This might be true, but remember inferences should be drawn from the information the author gives you!

If you chose D, you might be using the information that Mark Zuckerberg is worth over 28 billion dollars. It would be easy for him to pay others to design new sites, but remember, you need to use context clues! He is very wealthy, but that statement was giving you information about how successful Facebook was—not suggesting that he paid others to design more sites!

So remember, drawing inferences and conclusions is simply about using the information you are given to make an educated guess. You do this every single day so don't let this concept scare you. Look for the context clues, make sure they support your claim, and you'll be able to make accurate inferences and conclusions!

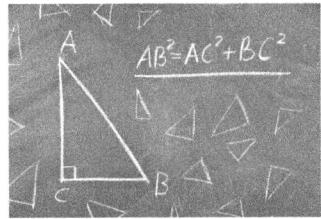

MATHEMATICS

THIS SECTION CONTAINS A SELF-ASSESSMENT AND MATH TUTORIALS. The tutorials are designed to familiarize general principles and the self-assessment contains general questions similar to the math questions likely to be on the ISEE® exam, but are not intended to be identical to the exam questions. The tutorials are not designed to be a complete math course, and it is assumed that students have some familiarity with math. If you do not understand parts of the tutorial, or find the tutorial difficult, it is recommended that you seek out additional instruction.

Tour of the ISEE Mathematics Content

The ISEE® mathematics section has 45 questions. Below is a detailed list of the mathematics topics likely to appear on the ISEE®. Make sure that you understand these topics at the very minimum.

- Convert decimals, percent and fractions

- Solve word problems

- Calculate percent and ratio

- Operations using fractions, percent and fractions

- Geometry and measurement

- Understand and solve simple algebra problems

The questions in the self-assessment are not the same as you will find on the ISEE® - that would be too easy! And nobody knows what the questions will be and they change all the time. Mostly, the changes consist of substituting new questions for old, but the changes also can be new question formats or styles, changes to the number of questions in each section, changes to the time limits for each section, and combining sections. So, while the format and exact wording of the questions may differ slightly, and changes from year to year, if you can answer the questions below, you will have no problem with the mathematics section of the ISEE®.

Mathematics Self-Assessment

The purpose of the self-assessment is:

- Identify your strengths and weaknesses.
- Develop your personalized study plan (above)
- Get accustomed to the ISEE® format
- Extra practice – the self-assessments are almost a full 3rd practice test!
- Provide a baseline score for preparing your study schedule.

Since this is a Self-assessment, and depending on how confident you are with Math, timing yourself is optional. The ISEE® has 45 questions, to be answered in 40 minutes. This self-assessment has 40 questions, so allow about 40 minutes to complete.

Once complete, use the table below to assess your understanding of the content, and prepare your study schedule described in chapter 1.

80% - 100%	Excellent – you have mastered the content
60 – 79%	Good. You have a working knowledge. Even though you can just pass this section, you may want to review the tutorials and do some extra practice to see if you can improve your mark.
40% - 59%	Below Average. You do not understand the content. Review the tutorials, and retake this quiz again in a few days, before proceeding to the practice test questions.
Less than 40%	Poor. You have a very limited understanding. Please review the tutorials, and retake this quiz again in a few days, before proceeding to the practice test questions.

Mathematics Self-Assessment Answer Sheet

	A	B	C	D	E		A	B	C	D	E
1	○	○	○	○	○	21	○	○	○	○	○
2	○	○	○	○	○	22	○	○	○	○	○
3	○	○	○	○	○	23	○	○	○	○	○
4	○	○	○	○	○	24	○	○	○	○	○
5	○	○	○	○	○	25	○	○	○	○	○
6	○	○	○	○	○	26	○	○	○	○	○
7	○	○	○	○	○	27	○	○	○	○	○
8	○	○	○	○	○	28	○	○	○	○	○
9	○	○	○	○	○	29	○	○	○	○	○
10	○	○	○	○	○	30	○	○	○	○	○
11	○	○	○	○	○	31	○	○	○	○	○
12	○	○	○	○	○	32	○	○	○	○	○
13	○	○	○	○	○	33	○	○	○	○	○
14	○	○	○	○	○	34	○	○	○	○	○
15	○	○	○	○	○	35	○	○	○	○	○
16	○	○	○	○	○	36	○	○	○	○	○
17	○	○	○	○	○	37	○	○	○	○	○
18	○	○	○	○	○	38	○	○	○	○	○
19	○	○	○	○	○	39	○	○	○	○	○
20	○	○	○	○	○	40	○	○	○	○	○

Math Self-Assessment

1. A boy has 5 red balls, 3 white balls and 2 yellow balls. What percent of the balls are yellow?

   a. 2%
   b. 8%
   c. 20%
   d. 12%

2. The length of a rectangle is twice of its width and its area is equal to the area of a square of side 12 cm. What will be the perimeter of the rectangle near to the nearest whole number?

   a. 36 cm
   b. 46 cm
   c. 51 cm
   d. 56 cm

3. There are 15 yellow and 35 orange balls in a basket. How many more yellow balls must be added to make yellow balls 65%?

   a. 35
   b. 50
   c. 65
   d. 70

4. At the beginning of 2009, Marilyn invested $5,000 in a savings account. The account pays 4% interest per year. At the end of the year, after the interest was paid, how much did Marilyn have in the account?

   a. $5,200
   b. $5,020
   c. $5,110
   d. $7,000

5. The average weight of 13 students in a class of 15 (two were absent that day) is 42 kg. When the remaining 2 were weighed, the average became 42.7 kg. If one of the remaining students weighs 48, how much does the other weigh?

   a. 44.7 kg.
   b. 45.6 kg.
   c. 46.5 kg.
   d. 47.4 kg.

6. The total expense of building a fence around a square field is $2000 at a rate of $5 per meter. What is the length of one side?

   a. 40 meters
   b. 80 meters
   c. 100 meters
   d. 320 meters

7. Convert 23.67 to percent.

   a. 2.367%
   b. 236.7%
   c. 23.67%
   d. 2367%

8. If 144 students need to go on a trip and the buses carry 36 students each, how many buses do they need?

   a. 6
   b. 5
   c. 4
   d. 3

9. A mother is making spaghetti for her son. The recipe calls for 500 grams of spaghetti, and 0.75 grams of salt. However, the mom just wants 125 grams of spaghetti. How much salt should she use?

    a. 0.38 grams
    b. 0.75 grams
    c. 0.19 grams
    d. 0.25 grams

10. A young student deposits $200 in a savings account hoping to buy a bicycle worth $245. If the bank offers a 15% interest rate, how long will the boy have to wait?

    a. 1½ years
    b. 2 ½ years
    c. 2 years
    d. 1 year

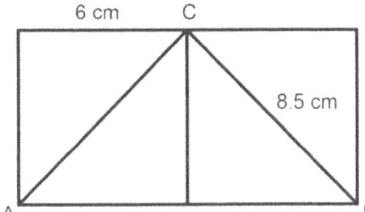

Note: figure not drawn to scale

11. Assuming the 2 quadrangles above are identical rectangles, what is perimeter of △ABC in the above shape?

    a. 25.5 cm
    b. 27 cm
    c. 30 cm
    d. 29 cm

12. A pet store had total sales of $19,304.56 for the month of June. If the wholesale cost was $5,284.34, the employees were paid $8,384.76, and the rent was $2,920.00, how much profit did the store make in June?

    a. $5,635.46
    b. $2,714.47
    c. $14,020.22
    d. $10,019.80

13. Tony bought 15 dozen eggs for $80. 16 eggs were broken during loading and unloading. He sold the remainder for $0.54 each. What will be his percentage profit? Provide answer in 2 significant digits.

    a. 11%
    b. 11.2%
    c. 11.5%
    d. 12%

14. The sale price of a car is $12,590, which is 20% off the original price. What is the original price?

    a. $14,310.40
    b. $14,990.90
    c. $15,108.00
    d. $15,737.50

15. Estimate 16 x 230.

    a. 31,000
    b. 301,000
    c. 3,100
    d. 3,000,000

16. In a small village there are 9 families with 3 children, 8 families with 2 children, and 4 families having 5 children. What is the average number of children in a family?

    a. 2.5
    b. 2.8
    c. 3
    d. 3.5

17. A goat eats 214 kg. of hay in 60 days, while a cow eats the same amount in 15 days. How long will it take to eat this hay together?

    a. 37.5
    b. 75
    c. 12
    d. 15

18. Sarah weighs 25 pounds more than Tony. If together they weigh 205 pounds, how much does Sarah weigh approximately in kilograms? Assume 1 pound = 0.4535 kilograms

    a. 41
    b. 48
    c. 50
    d. 52

19. Ann went from point A to point B. At the same time, Peter went from point B to point A. In 6 hours, they met, and in 3 more hours, Peter reached B. How many hours did it take Ann to travel from A to B?

    a. 18
    b. 9
    c. 15
    d. 12

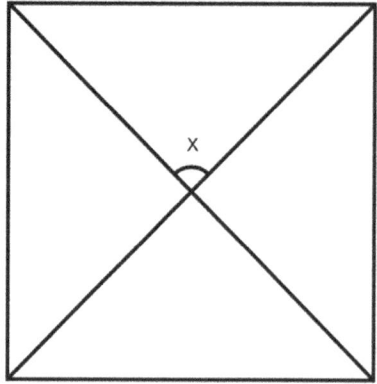

20. What is measurement of the indicated angle?

    a. 45°
    b. 90°
    c. 60°
    d. 30°

21. Mr. White wants to tile his rectangular backyard, which is 16 m × 11 m. The dimensions of each tile are 7 cm × 4 cm. If cost of each tile is $0.30 and 2.5% tiles break during handling, then what will be the total cost?

    a. $19234
    b. $20240
    c. $20895
    d. $21563

22. Translate the following into an equation: six times a number plus five.

    a. 6X + 5
    b. 6(X+5)
    c. 5X + 6
    d. (6 * 5) + 5

23. In the Euro cup football game, England won gold, Spain won silver and Holland won bronze medals. The three winners share the total prize money of $605,500 in the ratio of 4:2:1. How much money did Spain win?

    a. $86,500
    b. $173,000
    c. $201,830
    d. $346,000

24. Solve for b. $7 - 8b = 11 - 10b$.

    a. 2
    b. 3
    c. 5
    d. 6

25. A building is 15 m long and 20 m wide and 10 m high. What is the volume of the building?

    a. 45 m³
    b. 3,000 m³
    c. 1500 m³
    d. 300 m³

26. Solve 3/4 + 2/4 + 1.2

    a. 1 1/7
    b. 2 3/4
    c. 2 9/20
    d. 3 1/4

27. 3 boys are asked to clean a surface that is 4 ft². If the portion is divided equally among the boys, what size will each of them clean?

    a. 1 ft 6 inches
    b. 14 inches
    c. 1 ft 2 inches
    d. 1 ft² 48 in²

28. Great Britain has a Value-added tax of 15%. A shop sells a camera for $545. If the VAT is included in the price, what is the actual cost of the camera?

    a. $490.40
    b. $473.91
    c. $505.00
    d. $503.15

29. Simplify 0.12 + 1 2/5 − 1 3/5

    a. 1 1/25
    b. 1 3/25
    c. 1 2/5
    d. 2 3/5

30. A rectangular box measures 10 cm long and 8 cm wide and 10 cm high. What is the volume of the box?

    a. 28 cm³
    b. 2000 cm³
    c. 400 cm³
    d. 800 cm³

31. 5 men have to share a load weighing 10 kg 550 g equally among themselves. How much weight will each man have to carry?

    a. 900 g
    b. 1.5 kg
    c. 3 kg
    d. 2 kg 110 g

32. A worker's weekly salary was increased by 30%. If his new salary is $150, what was his old salary?

  a. $120.00
  b. $99.15
  c. $109.00
  d. $115.38

33. Estimate 46,227 + 101,032.

  a. 14,700
  b. 147,000
  c. 14,700,000
  d. 104,700

34. 2/15 ÷ 4/5 =

  a. 6/65
  b. 6/75
  c. 5/12
  d. 1/6

35. If Tim deposits $5,500 in a savings account that offers a 5% interest, what will be the total amount in his savings account after 3 years?

  a. $6,225
  b. $6,0325
  c. $325
  d. $6,325

36. The price of a product was increased by 45%. If the initial cost was $220, what is the new cost?

  a. $230
  b. $300
  c. $319
  d. $245

37. A map uses a scale of 1:2,000 How much distance on the ground is 5.2 inches on the map if the scale is in inches?

  a. 100,400
  b. 10, 500
  c. 10,400
  d. 10,400

38. Find 2 numbers that sum to 21 and the sum of the squares is 261.

  a. 14 and 7
  b. 15 and 6
  c. 16 and 5
  d. 17 and 4

39. Using the factoring method, solve the quadratic equation: $2x^2 - 3x = 0$

  a. 0 and 1.5
  b. 1.5 and 2
  c. 2 and 2.5
  d. 0 and 2

40. 2623 / 61 =

  a. 33
  b. 44
  c. 43
  d. 23

Answer Key

1. C
Total number of balls = 10, number of yellow balls = 2, so, 2/10 X 100 = 20%

2. C
Area of the square = 12 × 12 = 144 cm². Let x be the width so 2x will be the length of rectangle. The area will be 2 x 2 and the perimeter will be 2(2x + x) = 6x. According to the condition 2 x 2 = 144 then x = 8.48 cm. The perimeter will be 6 × 8.48 = 50.88 = 51 cm.

3. B
There are 50 balls in the basket now. Let x be the yellow balls that are to be added to make it 65%. So the equation becomes X + 15 /X + 50 = 65/100. X = 50.

4. A
5000 X 4% = 200
5000 + 200 = $5200

5. C
Total weight of 13 students with average 42 will be = 42 × 13 = 546 kg. Total weight of 15 students with average 42.7 will be = 42.7 × 15 = 640.5 kg. So the total weight of the remaining 2 will be = 640.5 - 546 = 94.5 kg. Weight of the other will be = 94.5 – 48 = 46.5 kg

6. C
Total length of the fence will be = 2000/5 = 400 meters. This will be equal to the perimeter of the square field, so the length of one side will be = 400/4 = 100 meters.

7. D
To convert to percent, simply multiply the decimal by 100 or move the decimal point 2 places to the right. Therefore, 23.67 x 100 = 2367%

8. C
144 ÷ 36 = 4

9. C
125: 500 is the same as 25 : 100 or 1 : 4. So the amount of salt will be 0.75/4 = 0.1875, or about .19 grams.

10. A
$200 invested at 15% per year will yield $30 interest at the end of the first year. For the second year the interest will be 34.50, so it will take about 1 1/2 years before he can buy the bike.

11. D
Perimeter of triangle ABC is asked.

Perimeter of a triangle = sum of all three sides.

Here, Perimeter of $\triangle ABC$ = |AC| + |CB| + |AB|.

Since the triangle is located in the middle of two adjacent and identical rectangles, we find the side lengths using these rectangles:

|AB| = 6 + 6 = 12 cm

|CB| = 8.5 cm

|AC| = |CB| = 8.5 cm

Perimeter = |AC| + |CB| + |AB| = 8.5 + 8.5 + 12 = 29 cm

12. A
19304.56 – 5284.34 – 8384.76 = 5635.46

13. A
Let us first mention the money Tony spent: $80

Now we need to find the money Tony earned:

He had 15 dozen eggs = 15•12 = 180 eggs. 16 eggs were broken. So,

Remaining number of eggs that Tony sold = 180 – 16 = 164.

Total amount he earned for selling 164 eggs = 164•0.54 = $88.56.

As a summary, he spent $80 and earned $88.56.

The profit is the difference: 88.56 - 80 = $8.56

Percentage profit is found by proportioning the profit to the money he spent:

8.56•100/80 = 10.7%

Checking the answers, we round 10.7 to the nearest whole number: 11%

14. D
Let the original price = x,
80/100 = 12590/X,
80X = 1259000,
X = 15737.50.

15. C
16 X 230 = 3680, or about 3100.

16. C
Let X = total number of families
Y = total number of children
Y = 9 x 3 + 8 x 2 + 4 x 5 = 63 and
X = 9 + 8 + 4 = 21
Average number of children in a family = Y/X = 63/21 = 3

17. C
Total hay = 214 kg,
The goat eats at a rate of 214/60 days = 3.6 kg per day.
The cow eats at a rate of 214/15 = 14.3 kg per day,
Together they eat 3.6 + 14.3 = 17.9 per day.
At a rate of 17.9 kg per day, they will consume 214 kg in 214/17.9 = 11.96 or 12 days approx.

18. D
Let us denote Sarah's weight by "x". Then, since she weighs 25 pounds more than Tony, Tony will be x-25. They together weigh 205 pounds which means that the sum of the two representations will be equal to 205:

Sarah : x

Tony : x - 25

x + (x - 25) = 205 ... by arranging this equation we have:

x + x - 25 = 205

2x - 25 = 205 ... we add 25 to each side to have x term alone:

2x - 25 + 25 = 205 + 25

2x = 230

x = 230/2

x = 115 pounds -> Sarah weighs 115 pounds. Since 1 pound is 0.4535 kilograms, we need to multiply 115 by 0.4535 to have her weight in kilograms:

x = 115 • 0.4535 = 52.1525 kilograms -> this is equal to 52 when rounded to the nearest whole number.

19. D
It took peter 3 hours to cover the distance Ann traveled in 6 hours (from point of meeting to point A, where Ann started). This means Peter is traveling at twice the speed of Ann. If it took peter 6 hours to reach the point of meeting, it will take Ann twice that long to get to Peter's point of origin = 6 x 2 = 12

20. A
The diagonals of a square intersect at right angles, so each angle measures 90° Half of that angle will be 45°

21. A
The area of each tile is 7 cm X 4 cm = 28 cm². The area of the yard is 16 m X 11 m = 176 m² = 1760000 cm². The number of tiles required is 1760000/28 = 62858. 2% of the tiles break during handling, so 1.02 X 62858 = 64115. Total cost will be 64115 X 0.3 = $19234.55.

22. B
Six times a number plus five is the same as saying six times (a number plus five). Or, 6 * (a number plus five). Let X be the number so, 6(X+5).

23. B
Spain won second prize so their ratio is 2/7
2/7 * 60550 = $173,000

24. A
7 − 8b = 11 − 10b. Bring same terms to same side of the equation by changing the negative or positive signs when they cross over, therefore -8b + 10b = 11 − 7, 2b = 4, b = 4/2 = 2

25. B
Formula for volume of a shape is L x W x H = 15 x 20 x 10 = 3,000 m³

26. C
3/4 + 2/4 + 1.2, first convert the decimal to fraction, = 3/4 + 2/4 + 1 1/5 = ¾ + 2/4 + 6/5 = (find common denominator) (15 + 10 + 24)/20 = 49/20 = 2 9/20

27. D
1 foot is equal to 12 inches. So 1 ft² = 12•12 in²
4 ft² = 4•12•12 in² = 576 in²

This amount of surface area is divided equally among 3 boys.

Each boy will clean 576/3 = 192 in²

192 in² = 144 in² + 48 in²; 144 in² = 1 ft²

So, each boy will clean 1 ft² and 48 in²

28. B
Actual cost = X, therefore, 545 = x + 0.15x, 545 = 1x + 0.15x, 545 = 1.15x, x = 545/1.15 = 473.91

29. B
0.12 + 2/5 + 3a/5, Convert decimal to fraction to get 3/25 + 2/5 + 3/5, = (3 + 10 + 15)/25, = 28/25 = 1 3/25

30. D
Formula for volume of a shape is L x W x H = 10 x 8 x 10 = 800 cm³

31. D
First convert the unit of measurements to be the same. Since 1000 g = 1 kg, 10 kg = 10 x 1000 = 10,000 + 550 g = 10,550 g. Divide 10,550 among 5 = 10550/5 = 2110 = 2 kg 110 g

32. D
Let old salary = X, therefore $150 = x + 0.30x, 150 = 1x + 0.30x, 150 = 1.30x, x = 150/1.30 = 115.38

33. B
46,227 + 101,032 is about 147,000. The actual total is 147,259.

34. D
To divide fractions, multiply the first fraction with the inverse of the second fraction. 2/15 x 5/4, (cancel out) = 1/3 x 1/2 = 1/6

35. D
P = $5,500, t = 3 years, r = 5%, I = ?
convert rate to decimal and 5% = 0.05
I = 5,500 x 0.05 x 3 = 825. Total amount in the account = principal + interest or 5,500 + 825 = $6,325

36. C
Initial cost was $220. new cost = 220 + 45% of 220, 45/100 x 220 = 99, therefore new price is 220 + 99 = $319.

37. C
1 inch on map = 2,000 inches on ground. So 5.2 inches on map = 5.2 x 2,000 = 10,400 inches on ground.

38. B
There are two statements made. This means that we can write two equations according to these statements: The sum of two numbers are 21: x + y = 21

The sum of the squares is 261: $x^2 + y^2$ = 261

We are asked to find x and y.

Since we have the sums of the numbers and the sums of their squares; we can use the square formula of x + y, that is:

$(x + y)^2 = x^2 + 2xy + y^2$ ... Here, we can insert the known values x + y and $x^2 + y^2$:

$(21)^2$ = 261 + 2xy ... Arranging to find xy:

441 = 261 + 2xy

441 - 261 = 2xy

180 = 2xy

xy = 180/2

xy = 90

We need to find two number which multiply to 90. Checking the answer choices, we see that in (b), 15 and 6 are given. 15•6 = 90. Also their squares sum up to 261 ($15^2 + 6^2$ = 225 + 36 = 261). So these two numbers satisfy the equation.

39. A
$2x^2 - 3x = 0$ ... we see that both of the terms contain x; so we can take it out as a factor:

x(2x - 3) = 0 ... two terms are multiplied and the result is zero. This means that either of the terms or both of the terms can be equal to zero:

x = 0 ... this is one solution

2x - 3 = 0 -> 2x = 3 -> x = 3/2 -> x = 1.5 ... this is the second solution.

So, the solutions are 0 and 1.5.

40. C
2623 / 61 = 43

How to Solve Word Problems

Most students find math word problems difficult. Tackling word problems is much easier if you have a systematic approach which we outline below.

Here is the biggest tip for studying word problems.

Practice regularly and systematically. Sounds simple and easy right? Yes it is, and yes it really does work.

Word problems are a way of thinking and require you to translate a real word problem into mathematical terms.

Some math instructors go so far as to say that learning how to think mathematically is the main reason for teaching word problems.

So what do we mean by Practice regularly and systematically? Studying word problems and math in general requires a logical and mathematical frame of mind. The only way you can get this is by practicing regularly, which means everyday.

It is critical that you practice word problems everyday for the 5 days before the exam as a bare minimum.

If you practice and miss a day, you have lost the mathematical frame of mind and the benefit of your previous practice is pretty much gone. Anyone who has done any amount of math will agree – you have to practice everyday.

Everything is important. The other critical point about word problems is that all of the information given in the problem has some purpose. There is no unnecessary information! Word problems are typically around 50 words in 1 to 3 sentences. If the sometimes complicated relationships are to be explained in that short an explanation, every word has to count. Make sure that you use every piece of information.

Here are 9 simple steps to solve word problems.

Step 1 – Read through the problem at least three times. The first reading should be a quick scan, and the next two readings should be done slowly with a view to finding answers to these important questions:

What does the problem ask? (Usually located towards the end of the problem)

What does the problem imply? (This is usually a point you were asked to remember).

Mark all information, and underline all important words or phrases.

Step 2 – Try to make a pictorial representation of the problem such as a circle and an arrow to indicate travel. This makes the problem a bit more real and sensible to you.

A favorite word problem is something like, 1 train leaves Station A travelling at 100 km/hr and another train leaves Station B travelling at 60 km/hr. ...

Draw a line, the two stations, and the two trains at either end. This will help solidify the situation in your mind.

Step 3 – Use the information you have to make a table with a blank portion to indicate information you do not know.

Step 4 – Assign a single letter to represent each unknown data in your table. You can write down the unknown that each letter represents so that you do not make the error of assigning answers to the wrong unknown, because a word problem may have multiple unknowns and you will need to create equations for each unknown.

Step 5 – Translate the English terms in the word problem into a mathematical algebraic equation. Remember that the main problem with word problems is that they are not expressed in regular math equations. You ability to correctly identify the variables and translate the word problem into an equation determines your ability to solve the problem.

Step 6 – Check the equation to see if it looks like regular equations that you are used to seeing and whether it looks sensible. Does the equation appear to represent the information in the question? Take note that you may need to re-write some formulas needed to solve the word problem equation. For example, word distance problems may need you rewriting the distance formula, which is Distance = Time x Rate. If the word problem requires that you solve for time you will need to use Distance/Rate and Distance/Time to solve for Rate. If you understand the distance word problem you should be able to identify the variable you need to solve for.

Step 7 – Use algebra rules to solve the derived equation. Take note that the laws of equation demands that what is done on this side of the equation has to also be done on the other side. You have to solve the equation so that the unknown ends up alone on one side. Where there are multiple unknowns you will need to use elimination or substitution methods to resolve all the equations.

Step 8 – Check your final answers to see if they make sense with the information given in the problem. For example if the word problem involves a discount, the final price should be less or if a product was taxed then the final answer has to cost more.

Step 9 – Cross check your answers by placing the answer or answers in the first equation to replace the unknown or unknowns. If your answer is correct then both side of the equation must equate or equal. If your answer is not correct then you may have derived a wrong equation or solved the equation wrongly. Repeat the necessary steps to correct.

Types of Word Problems

Word problems can be classified into 12 types. Below are examples of each type with a complete solution. Some types of word problems can be solved quickly using multiple choice strategies and some cannot. Always look for ways to estimate the answer and then eliminate choices.

1. Age

A girl is 10 years older than her brother. By next year, she will be twice the age of her brother. What are their ages now?

    a. 25, 15
    b. 19, 9
    c. 21, 11
    d. 29, 19

Solution: B

We will assume that the girl's age is "a" and her brother's is "b." This means that based on the information in the first sentence,
a = 10 + b

Next year, she will be twice her brother's age, which gives
a + 1 = 2(b+1)

We need to solve for one unknown factor and then use the answer to solve for the other. To do this we substitute the value of "a" from the first equation into the second equation. This gives

10+b + 1 = 2b + 2
11 + b = 2b + 2
11 − 2 = 2b − b
b= 9

9 = b this means that her brother is 9 years old. Solving for the girl's age in the first equation gives a = 10 + 9. a = 19 the girl is aged 19. So, the girl is aged 19 and the boy is 9

2. Distance or speed

Two boats travel down a river towards the same destination, starting at the same time. One boat is traveling at 52 km/hr, and the other boat at 43 km/hr. How far apart will they be after 40 minutes?

    a. 46.67 km
    b. 19.23 km
    c. 6.0 km
    d. 14.39 km

Solution: C

After 40 minutes, the first boat will have traveled = 52 km/hr x 40 minutes/60 minutes = 34.66 km
After 40 minutes, the second boat will have traveled = 43 km/hr x 40/60 minutes = 28.66 km
Difference between the two boats will be 34.66 km – 28.66 km = 6 km.

Multiple Choice Strategy

First estimate the answer. The first boat is travelling 9 km. faster than the second, for 40 minutes, which is 2/3 of an hour. 2/3 of 9 = 6, as a rough guess of the distance apart.

Choices A, B and D can be eliminated right away.

3. Ratio

The instructions in a cookbook states that 700 grams of flour must be mixed in 100 ml of water, and 0.90 grams of salt added. A cook however has just 325 grams of flour. What is the quantity of water and salt that he should use?

 a. 0.41 grams and 46.4 ml
 b. 0.45 grams and 49.3 ml
 c. 0.39 grams and 39.8 ml
 d. 0.25 grams and 40.1 ml

Solution: A

The Cookbook states 700 grams of flour, but the cook only has 325. The first step is to determine the percentage of flour he has 325/700 x 100 = 46.4%
That means that 46.4% of all other items must also be used.
46.4% of 100 = 46.4 ml of water
46.4% of 0.90 = 0.41 grams of salt.

Multiple Choice Strategy

The recipe calls for 700 grams of flour but the cook only has 325, which is just less than half, the quantity of water and salt are going to be about half.

Choices C and D can be eliminated right away. Choice B is very close so be careful. Looking closely at Choice B, it is exactly half, and since 325 is slightly less than half of 700, it can't be correct.

Choice A is correct.

4. Percent

An agent received $6,685 as his commission for selling a property. If his commission was 13% of the selling price, how much was the property?

   a. $68,825
   b. $121,850
   c. $49,025
   d. $51,423

Solution: D

Let's assume that the property price is x
That means from the information given, 13% of x = 6,685
Solve for x,
x = 6685 x 100/13 = $51,423

Multiple Choice Strategy

The commission,13%, is just over 10%, which is easier to work with. Round up $6685 to $6700, and multiple by 10 for an approximate answer. 10 X 6700 = $67,000. You can do this in your head. Choice B is much too big and can be eliminated. Choice C is too small and can be eliminated. Choices A and D are left and good possibilities.

Do the calculations to make the final choice.

5. Sales & Profit

A store owner buys merchandise for $21,045. He transports them for $3,905 and pays his staff $1,450 to stock the merchandise on his shelves. If he does not incur further costs, how much does he need to sell the items to make $5,000 profit?

   a. $32,500
   b. $29,350
   c. $32,400
   d. $31,400

Solution: D

Total cost of the items is $21,045 + $3,905 + $1,450 = $26,400
Total cost is now $26,400 + $5000 profit = $31,400

Multiple Choice Strategy

Round off and add the numbers up in your head quickly.
21,000 + 4,000 + 1500 = 26500. Add in 5000 profit for a total of 31500.

Choice B is too small and can be eliminated. Choice C and Choice A are too large and can be eliminated.

6. Tax/Income

A woman earns $42,000 per month and pays 5% tax on her monthly income. If the Government increases her monthly taxes by $1,500, what is her income after tax?

    a. $38,400
    b. $36,050
    c. $40,500
    d. $39, 500

Solution: A

Initial tax on income was 5/100 x 42,000 = $2,100
$1,500 was added to the tax to give $2,100 + 1,500 = $3,600
Income after tax left is $42,000 - $3,600 = $38,400

7. Interest

A man invests $3000 in a 2-year term deposit that pays 3% interest per year. How much will he have at the end of the 2-year term?

    a. $5,200
    b. $3,020
    c. $3,182.7
    d. $3,000

Solution: C

This is a compound interest problem. The funds are invested for 2 years and interest is paid yearly, so in the second year, he will earn interest on the interest paid in the first year.

3% interest in the first year = 3/100 x 3,000 = $90
At end of first year, total amount = 3,000 + 90 = $3,090
Second year = 3/100 x 3,090 = 92.7.
At end of second year, total amount = $3090 + $92.7 = $3,182.7

8. Averaging

The average weight of 10 books is 54 grams. 2 more books were added and the average weight became 55.4. If one of the 2 new books added weighed 62.8 g, what is the weight of the other?

    a. 44.7 g
    b. 67.4 g
    c. 62 g
    d. 52 g

Solution: C

Total weight of 10 books with average 54 grams will be=10×54=540 g
Total weight of 12 books with average 55.4 will be=55.4×12=664.8 g
So total weight of the remaining 2 will be= 664.8 – 540 = 124.8 g
If one weighs 62.8, the weight of the other will be= 124.8 g – 62.8 g = 62 g

Multiple Choice Strategy

Averaging problems can be estimated by looking at which direction the average goes. If additional items are added and the average goes up, the new items much be greater than the average. If the average goes down after new items are added, the new items must be less than the average.

Here, the average is 54 grams and 2 books are added which increases the average to 55.4, so the new books must weight more than 54 grams.

Choices A and D can be eliminated right away.

9. Probability

A bag contains 15 marbles of various colors. If 3 marbles are white, 5 are red and the rest are black, what is the probability of randomly picking out a black marble from the bag?

    a. 7/15
    b. 3/15
    c. 1/5
    d. 4/15

Solution: A

Total marbles = 15
Number of black marbles = 15 – (3 + 5) = 7
Probability of picking out a black marble = 7/15

10. Two Variables

A company paid a total of $2850 to book for 6 single rooms and 4 double rooms in a hotel for one night. Another company paid $3185 to book for 13 single rooms for one night in the same hotel. What is the cost for single and double rooms in that hotel?

    a. single= $250 and double = $345
    b. single= $254 and double = $350
    c. single = $245 and double = $305
    d. single = $245 and double = $345

Solution: D

We can determine the price of single rooms from the information given of the second company. 13 single rooms = 3185.
One single room = 3185 / 13 = 245
The first company paid for 6 single rooms at $245. 245 x 6 = $1470
Total amount paid for 4 double rooms by first company = $2850 - $1470 = $1380
Cost per double room = 1380 / 4 = $345

11. Geometry

The length of a rectangle is 5 in. more than its width. The perimeter of the rectangle is 26 in. What is the width and length of the rectangle?

    a. width = 6 inches, Length = 9 inches
    b. width = 4 inches, Length = 9 inches
    c. width =4 inches, Length = 5 inches
    d. width = 6 inches, Length = 11 inches

Solution: B

Formula for perimeter of a rectangle is 2(L + W)
p=26, so 2(L+W) = p
The length is 5 inches more than the width, so
2(w+5) + 2w = 26
2w + 10 + 2w = 26
2w + 2w = 26 - 10
4w = 16

W = 16/4 = 4 inches

L is 5 inches more than w, so L = 5 + 4 = 9 inches.

12. Totals and fractions

A basket contains 125 oranges, mangos and apples. If 3/5 of the fruits in the basket are mangos and only 2/5 of the mangos are ripe, how many ripe mangos are there in the basket?

    a. 30
    b. 68
    c. 55
    d. 47

Solution: A
Number of mangos in the basket is 3/5 x 125 = 75
Number of ripe mangos = 2/5 x 75 = 30

Fraction Tips, Tricks and Shortcuts

When you are writing an exam, time is precious, and anything you can do to answer questions faster, is a real advantage. Here are some ideas, shortcuts, tips and tricks that can speed up answering fraction problems.

Remember that a fraction is just a number which names a portion of something. For instance, instead of having a whole pie, a fraction says you have a part of a pie--such as a half of one or a fourth of one.

Two digits make up a fraction. The digit on top is known as the numerator. The digit on the bottom is known as the denominator. To remember which is which, just remember that "denominator" and "down" both start with a "d." And the "downstairs" number is the denominator. So for instance, in ½, the numerator is the 1 and the denominator (or "downstairs") number is the 2.

- It's easy to add two fractions if they have the same denominator. Just add the digits on top and leave the bottom one the same: 1/10 + 6/10 = 7/10.

- It's the same with subtracting fractions with the same denominator: 7/10 - 6/10 = 1/10.

- Adding and subtracting fractions with different denominators is a little more complicated. First, you have to get the problem so that they do have the same denominators. The easiest way to do this is to multiply the denominators: For 2/5 + 1/2 multiply 5 by 2. Now you have a denominator of 10. But now you have to change the top numbers too. Since you multiplied the 5 in 2/5 by 2, you also multiply the 2 by 2, to get 4. So the first number is now 4/10. Since you multiplied the second number times 5, you also multiply its top number by 5, to get a final fraction of 5/10. Now you can add 5 and 4 together to get a final sum of 9/10.

- Sometimes you'll be asked to reduce a fraction to its simplest form. This means getting it to where the only common factor of the numerator and denominator is 1. Think of it this way: Numerators and denominators are brothers that must be treated the same. If you do something to one, you must do it to the other, or it's just not fair. For instance, if you divide your numerator by 2, then you should also divide the denominator by the same. Let's take an example: The fraction 2/10. This is not reduced to its simplest terms because there is a number that will divide evenly into both: the number 2. We want to make it so that the only number that will divide evenly into both is 1. What can we divide into 2 to get 1? The number 2, of course! Now to be "fair," we have to do the same thing to the denominator: Divide 2 into 10 and you get 5. So our new, reduced fraction is 1/5.

- In some ways, multiplying fractions is the easiest of all: Just multiply the two top numbers and then multiply the two bottom numbers. For

instance, with this problem:
2/5 X 2/3 you multiply 2 by 2 and get a top number of 4; then multiply 5 by 3 and get a bottom number of 15. Your answer is 4/15.

- ☐ Dividing fractions is more involved, but not difficult. You once again multiply, but only AFTER you have turned the second fraction upside-down. To divide ⅞ by ½, turn the ½ into 2/1, then multiply the top numbers and multiply the bottom numbers: ⅞ X 2/1 gives us 14 on top and 8 on the bottom.

Converting Fractions to Decimals

There are a couple of ways to become good at converting fractions to decimals. One -- the one that will make you the fastest in basic math skills -- is to learn some basic fraction facts. It's a good idea, if you're good at memory, to memorize the following:

1/100 is one hundredth, or .01.

1/50 is two hundredths, or .02.

1/25 is one twenty-fifths or four hundredths, or .04.

1/20 is one twentieth or five hundredths, or .05.

1/10 is one tenth, or .1.

1/8 is one eighth, or one hundred twenty-five thousandths, or .125.

1/5 is one fifth, or two tenths, or .2.

1/4 is one fourth or twenty-five hundredths, or .25.

1/3 is one third or thirty-three hundredths, or .33.

1/2 is one half or five tenths, or .5.

3/4 is three fourths, or seventy-five hundredths, or .75.

Of course, if you're no good at memorization, another good technique for converting a fraction to a decimal is to manipulate it so that the fraction's denominator is 10, 10, 1000, or some other power of 10. Here's an example: We'll start with ¾. What is the first number in the 4 "times table" that you can multiply and get a multiple of 10? Can you multiply 4 by something to get 10? No. Can you multiply it by something to get 100? Yes! 4 X 25 is 100. So let's take that 25 and multiply it by the numerator in our fraction ¾. The numerator is 3, and 3 X 25 is 75. We'll move the decimal in 75 all the way to the left, and we find that ¾ is .75.

We'll do another one: 1/5. Again, we want to find a power of 10 that 5 goes into evenly. Will 5 go into 10? Yes! It goes 2 times. So we'll take that 2 and multiply it by our numerator, 1, and we get 2. We move the decimal in 2 all the way to the left and find that 1/5 is equal to .2.

Converting Fractions to Percent

Working with either fractions or percents can be intimidating enough. But converting from one to the other? That's a genuine nightmare for those who are not math wizards. However, it doesn't have to be that way. Here are two ways to make it easier and faster to convert a fraction to a percent.

- First, you might remember that a fraction is nothing more than a division problem: you're dividing the bottom number into the top number. So for instance, if we start with a fraction 1/10, we are making a division problem with the 10 on the outside the bracket and the 1 on the inside. As you remember from your lessons on dividing by decimals, since 10 won't go into 1, you add a decimal and make it 10 into 1.0. 10 into 10 goes 1 time, and since it's behind the decimal, it's .1. And how do we say .1? We say "one tenth," which is exactly what we started with: 1/10. So we have a number we can work with now: .1. When we're dealing with percents, though, we're dealing strictly with hundredths (not tenths). You remember from studying decimals that adding a zero to the right of the number on the right side of the decimal does not change the value. Therefore, we can change .1 into .10 and have the same number--except now it's expressed as hundredths. We have 10 hundredths. That's ten out of 100--which is just another way of saying ten percent (ten per hundred or ten out of 100). In other words .1 = .10 = 10 percent. Remember, if you're changing from a decimal to a percent, get rid of the decimal on the left and replace it with a percent mark on the right: 10%. Let's review those steps again: Divide 10 into 1. Since 10 doesn't go into 1, turn 1 into 1.0. Now divide 10 into 1.0. Since 10 goes into 10 1 time, put it there and add your decimal to make it .1. Since a percent is always "hundredths," let's change .1 into .10. Then remove the decimal on the left and replace with a percent sign on the right. The answer is 10%.

- If you're doing these conversions on a multiple-choice test, here's an idea that might be even easier and faster. Let's say you have a fraction of 1/8 and you're asked what the percent is. Since we know that "percent" means hundredths, ask yourself what number we can multiply 8 by to get 100. Since there is no number, ask what number gets us close to 100. That number is 12: 8 X 12 = 96. So it gets us a little less than 100. Now, whatever you do to the denominator, you have to do to the numerator. Let's multiply 1 X 12 and we get 12. However, since 96 is a little less than 100, we know that our answer will be a percent a little MORE than 12%. So if your possible answers on the multiple-choice test are these:

a) 8.5%   b) 19%   c) 12.5%   d) 25%

then we know the answer is c) 12.5%, because it's a little MORE than the 12 we got in our math problem above.

Another way to look at this, using multiple choice strategy is you know the answer will be "about" 12. Looking at the other choices, they are either too large or too small and can be eliminated right away.

This was an easy example to demonstrate, so don't be fooled! You probably won't get such an easy question on your exam, but the principle holds just the same. By estimating your answer quickly, you can eliminate choices immediately and save precious exam time.

Decimal Tips, Tricks and Shortcuts

Converting Decimals to Fractions

One of the most important tricks for correctly converting a decimal to a fraction doesn't involve math at all. It's simply to learn to say the decimal correctly. If you say "point one" or "point 25" for .1 and .25, you'll have more trouble getting the conversion correct. However, if you know that it's called "one tenth" and "twenty-five hundredths," you're on the way to a correct conversion. That's because, if you know your fractions, you know that "one tenth" looks like this: 1/10. And "twenty-five hundredths" looks like this: 25/100.

Even if you have digits before the decimal, such as 3.4, learning how to say the word will help you with the conversion into a fraction. It's not "three point four," it's "three and four tenths." Knowing this, you know that the fraction which looks like "three and four tenths" is 3 4/10.

Of course, your conversion is not complete until you reduce the fraction to its lowest terms: It's not 25/100, but 1/4.

Converting Decimals to Percent

Changing a decimal to a percent is easy if you remember one math formula: multiply by 100. For instance, if you start with .45, you change it to a percent by simply multiplying it by 100. You then wind up with 45. Add the % sign to the end and you get 45%.

That seems easy enough, right? Here think of it this way: You just take out the decimal and stick in a percent sign on the opposite sign. In other words, the decimal on the left is replaced by the % on the right.

It doesn't work that easily if the decimal is in the middle of the number. Let's use 3.7 for example. Here, take out the decimal in the middle and replace it with a 0 % at the end. So 3.7 converted to decimal is 370%.

Percent Tips, Tricks and Shortcuts

Percent problems are not nearly as scary as they appear, if you remember this neat trick:

Draw a cross as in:

Portion	Percent
Whole	100

In the upper left, write PORTION. In the bottom left write WHOLE. In the top right, write PERCENT and in the bottom right, write 100. Whatever your problem is, you will leave blank the unknown, and fill in the other four parts. For example, let's suppose your problem is: Find 10% of 50. Since we know the 10% part, we put 10 in the percent corner. Since the whole number in our problem is 50, we put that in the corner marked whole. You always put 100 underneath the percent, so we leave it as is, which leaves only the top left corner blank. This is where we'll put our answer. Now simply multiply the two corner numbers that are NOT 100. Here, it's 10 X 50. That gives us 500. Now multiply this by the remaining corner, or 100, to get a final answer of 5. 5 is the number that goes in the upper-left corner, and is your final solution. Another hint to remember: Percents are the same thing as hundredths in decimals. So .45 is the same as 45 hundredths or 45 percent.

Converting Percents to Decimals

Percents are simply a specific type of decimals, so it should be no surprise that converting between the two is actually fairly simple. Here are a few tricks and shortcuts to keep in mind:

- Remember that percent literally means "per 100" or "for every 100." So when you speak of 30% you're saying 30 for every 100 or the fraction 30/100. In basic math, you learned that fractions that have 10 or 100 as the denominator can easily be turned into a decimal. 30/100 is thirty hundredths, or expressed as a decimal, .30.
- Another way to look at it: To convert a percent to a decimal, simply

divide the number by 100. So for instance, if the percent is 47%, divide 47 by 100. The result will be .47. Get rid of the % mark and you're done.
- Remember that the easiest way of dividing by 100 is by moving your decimal two spots to the left.

Converting Percents to Fractions

Converting percents to fractions is easy. After all, a percent is nothing except a type of fraction; it tells you what part of 100 that you're talking about. Here are some simple ideas for making the conversion from a percent to a fraction:

- If the percent is a whole number -- say 34% -- then simply write a fraction with 100 as the denominator (the bottom number). Then put the percentage itself on top. So 34% becomes 34/100.
- Now reduce as you would reduce any percent. Here, by dividing 2 into 34 and 2 into 100, you get 17/50.
- If your percent is not a whole number -- say 3.4% --then convert it to a decimal expressed as hundredths. 3.4 is the same as 3.40 (or 3 and forty hundredths). Now ask yourself how you would express "three and forty hundredths" as a fraction. It would, of course, be 3 40/100. Reduce this and it becomes 3 2/5.

How to Answer Basic Math Multiple Choice

Math is the one section where you need to make sure that you understand the processes before you ever tackle it. That's because the time allowed on the math portion is typically so short that there's not much room for error. You have to be fast and accurate. It's imperative that before the test day arrives, you've learned all of the main formulas that will be used, and then to create your own problems (and solve them).

On the actual test day, use the "Plug-Check-Check" strategy. Here's how it goes.

Read the problem, but not the answers. You'll want to work the problem first and come up with your own answers. If you did the work right, you should find your answer among the choices.

If you need help with the problem, plug actual numbers into the variables given. You'll find it easier to work with numbers than it is to work with letters. For instance, if the question asks, "If Y - 4 is 2 more than Z, then Y+5 is how much more than Z?" try selecting a value for Y. Let's take 6. Your question now becomes, "If 6-4 is 2 more than Z, then 6 plus 5 is how much more than Z?" Now your answer should be easier to work with.

Check the answer choices to see if your answer matches one of those. If so, select it.

If no answer matches the one you got, re-check your math, but this time, use a different method. In math, it's common for there to be more than one way to solve a problem. As a simple example, if you multiplied 12 X 13 and did not get an answer that matches one of the answer choices, you might try adding 13 together 12 different times and see if you get a good answer.

Math Multiple Choice Strategy

The two strategies for working with basic math multiple choice are Estimation and Elimination.

Math Strategy 1 - Estimation.

Just like it sounds, try to estimate an approximate answer first. Then look at the choices.

Math Strategy 2 - Elimination.

For every question, no matter what type, eliminating obviously incorrect answers narrows the possible choices. Elimination is probably the most powerful strategy for answering multiple choice.

Here are a few basic math examples of how this works.

Solve 2/3 + 5/12

    a. 9/17

    b. 3/11

    c. 7/12

    d. 1 1/12

First estimate the answer. 2/3 is more than half and 5/12 is about half, so the answer is going to be very close to 1.

Next, Eliminate. Choice A is about 1/2 and can be eliminated, choice B is very small, less than 1/2 and can be eliminated. Choice C is close to 1/2 and can be eliminated. Leaving only choice D, which is just over 1.

Work through the solution, a common denominator is needed, a number which both 3 and 12 will divide into.
2/3 = 8/12. So, 8+5/12 = 13/12 = 1 1/12

Choice D is correct.

Solve 4/5 − 2/3

    a. 2/2

    b. 2/13

    c. 1

    d. 2/15

You can eliminate choice A, because it is 1 and since both numbers are close to one, the difference is going to be very small. You can eliminate choice C for the same reason.

Next, look at the denominators. Since 5 and 3 don't go in to 13, you can eliminate choice B as well.

That leaves choice D.

Checking the answer, the common denominator will be 15. So 12-10/15 = 2/15. Choice D is correct.

Fractions shortcut - Cancelling out.

In any operation with fractions, if the numerator of one fractions has a common multiple with the denominator of the other, you can cancel out. This saves time and simplifies the problem quickly, making it easier to manage.

Solve 2/15 ÷ 4/5

    a. 6/65

    b. 6/75

    c. 5/12

    d. 1/6

To divide fractions, we multiply the first fraction with the inverse of the second fraction. Therefore we have 2/15 x 5/4. The numerator of the first fraction, 2, shares a multiple with the denominator of the second fraction, 4, which is 2. These cancel out, which gives, 1/3 x 1/2 = 1/6

Cancelling Out solved the questions very quickly, but we can still use multiple choice strategies to answer.

Choice B can be eliminated because 75 is too large a denominator. Choice C can be eliminated because 5 and 15 don't go into 12.

Choice D is correct.

Decimal Multiple Choice strategy and Shortcuts.

Multiplying decimals gives a very quick way to estimate and eliminate choices. Anytime that you multiply decimals, it is going to give an answer with the same number of decimal places as the combined operands.

So for example,

2.38 X 1.2 will produce a number with three places of decimal, which is 2.856.

Here are a few examples with step-by-step explanation:

Solve 2.06 x 1.2

    a. 24.82

    b. 2.482

    c. 24.72

    d. 2.472

This is a simple question, but even before you start calculating, you can eliminate several choices. When multiplying decimals, there will always be as many numbers behind the decimal place in the answer as the sum of the ones in the initial problem, so choice A and C can be eliminate.

The correct answer is D: 2.06 x 1.2 = 2.472

Solve 20.0 ÷ 2.5

    a. 12.05

    b. 9.25

    c. 8.3

    d. 8

First estimate the answer to be around 10, and eliminate choice A. And since it'd also be an even number, you can eliminate choice B and C., leaving only choice D.

The correct Answer is D: 20.0 ÷ 2.5 = 8

How to Write an Essay

Writing an essay can be a difficult process, especially if you are under time constraints such as during an exam. Here are three simple steps to help you to write a solid, well thought out essay:

1. Brainstorm potential themes and general ideas for your essay.

2. Outline your essay step by step, including subheadings for ease of understanding.

3. Write your essay carefully being aware of proper grammar and sentence structure.

Brainstorming

You should first spend some time thinking about the general subject of the essay. If the essay is asking a question, you must make sure to answer this fully in your essay. You may find it helpful to highlight key words in your assignment or use a simple spider diagram to jot down key ideas.

Example

Read the following information and complete the following assignment:

Joseph Conrad is a Polish author who lived in England for most of his life and wrote a prolific amount of English literature. Much of his work was completed during the height of the British Empire's colonial imperialism.

Assignment: What impact has Joseph Conrad had on modern society? Present your point of view on the matter and support it with evidence. Your evidence may include reasoning, logic, examples from readings, your own experience, and observations.

Joseph Conrad

Background? sailor, adventure, Polish immigrant, Youth, Nostromo, Heart of Darkness
Themes in his works? ivory, silver trading, colonialism, corruption, greed
Thoughts? descent into madness, nature of evil

An outline or plan is critical to organize your thoughts and ideas fully and logically. There are many ways to do this; the easiest is to write down the following headings:

1. Title
2. Introduction
3. Body
4. Conclusion

You should then jot down key ideas and themes that fit logically under the appropriate heading. This plan is now the backbone of your essay.

Tip: Even if you are not required to produce an outline or plan for the assignment, you should always leave it with your essay in the exam booklet or the back of the assignment paper. Simply draw a line across it and write 'plan' or 'outline'. This demonstrates to the reader the approach you use in formulating and finally writing your essay.

Writing the essay

Your introduction is what will help the reader to decide whether they want to read the rest of your essay. The introduction also introduces the subject matter and allows you to provide a general background to the reader. The first sentence is very important and you should avoid starting the essay with openers such as 'I will be comparing…'

Example Essay 1

> Born as Józef Teodor Konrad Korzeniowski on December 3rd, 1857, Joseph Conrad led an adventurous life. As a Polish immigrant, Conrad never quite fit into England where he spent most of his adult life. As a younger man, Conrad made a living off sailing voyages. These swashbuckling experiences soon had him writing tales of the high seas such as one of his first works, Youth. While his early, adventurous work was of high quality, Conrad is best remembered for shedding light on the exploitative side of colonialism. Age and experience led him to start writing about (and challenging) the darker side of the imperial way of thinking. Conrad's work has forever soured words such as colonialism and imperialism.

In the main, or body of your essay, you should always be yourself and be original.

- Avoid using clichés.
- Be aware of your tone.
- Consider the language that you use. Avoid jargon and slang. Use clear prose and imagery.

- Your writing should always flow; remember to use transitions, especially between paragraphs. Read aloud in your head to make sure a paragraph sounds right.
- Always try to use a new paragraph for new ideas.

Example

> *Conrad's written fiction focused on themes such as greed and power. He portrayed these two concepts as purveyors of evil. Greed and power may take on different guises, but the result would always be the same.*
>
> *Perhaps his most famous piece, The Heart of Darkness, is about the descent of an English ivory trader, Mr. Kurtz, into madness. We are taken up a river resembling the Congo by a narrator, Marlow, who is sent to retrieve Mr. Kurtz. Marlow eventually finds that Kurtz has been diluted by power and greed, the two things that spurred on colonialism in Africa. Kurtz has taken charge of a large tribe of natives (that he brutalizes) and has been hoarding ivory for himself.*
>
> *Much of Conrad's later work was cut from the same vein as The Heart of Darkness. His crowning achievement is considered Nostromo where he takes an idealistic hero and corrupts him with colonial greed. Only this time the greed is for silver, not ivory.*
>
> *Conrad's work resonates with readers partly because it was semi-autobiographical. Where his experience sailing the high seas helped bring his adventure stories to light, likewise did his experience witnessing atrocities in Africa reverberate through his writing.*

The conclusion is your last chance to impress your reader and brings your entire essay to a logical close. You may want to link your conclusion back to your introduction or provide some closing statements. Do not panic if you cannot close your essay off completely. Few subjects offer closure.

Your conclusion should always be consistent with the rest of the essay and you should never introduce a new idea in your conclusion. It is also important to remember that a weak conclusion can diminish the impact of a good essay.

Example

> *In sum, Joseph Conrad's life experiences and masterful writing left a lasting impact on the image of progress and what it meant*
>
> *to "move forward." He brought to light the cost in human lives that*

was required for Europe to continue mining natural resources from foreign lands. Joseph Conrad had a permanent impact on imperial culture, and colonial brutality has been on the decline ever since his work was published.

Presentation

Poor grammar and punctuation can ruin an otherwise good essay. You should always follow any requirements about the presentation of your essay, such as word count. You should also make sure that your writing is legible. Always allow time for one final read-through before submission.

Tip: If you are able to, write with double spacing. If you make a mistake, you can cross it out and write the correction on the blank line above.

Some final points to think about for writing a solid, well thought out essay:

- A good essay will contain a strong focus.
- There is no set essay structure but you can use subheadings for better readability.
- Avoid particularly sensitive or controversial material. If you must write about something controversial, always make sure to include counter arguments.
- Your essay may have little to do with the subject itself; it is about what you make of the subject.
- Your essay can include examples from your readings, experience, studies or observations.
- Spend time doing practice essays and looking at sample essays beforehand.

Example Essay 2

How Community Service Benefits Both Individuals and Society

Introduction
Community service plays a crucial role in developing strong and supportive communities. Not only does it benefit the people who receive help, but it also offers numerous personal growth opportunities for those who volunteer. In this essay, I will discuss how community service provides benefits to both individuals and society, fostering a culture of giving and growth.

Commentary:

Thesis Statement: The thesis is clear and states the essay's main point, setting up the reader for the discussion of both individual and societal benefits of community service.

Hook/General Introduction: The first sentence grabs attention by introducing the broad topic of community service. It also offers a sense of why this subject matters.

Body Paragraph 1: The Personal Benefits of Community Service

One of the most significant advantages of community service for individuals is personal development. Volunteering can enhance a person's empathy, patience, and understanding of different social issues. For instance, by working at a homeless shelter, a volunteer gains insight into the challenges of homelessness and is better equipped to understand the importance of supporting social services. Additionally, community service can improve various skills, including communication, teamwork, and leadership. This is particularly true for high school students who participate in volunteer activities, as they often find themselves in leadership roles that challenge them to grow personally and professionally.

Commentary:

Topic Sentence: The paragraph starts with a clear topic sentence that introduces the focus on the personal benefits of community service.

Supporting Details and Examples: Specific examples, like volunteering at a homeless shelter, are used to support the topic sentence and add depth to the argument.
Explanation and Analysis: The paragraph analyzes the benefits, explaining how community service leads to skill-building and personal growth.

Body Paragraph 2: The Societal Benefits of Community Service

In addition to benefiting individuals, community service also strengthens society as a whole. When people engage in community service, they help build a more connected and caring society. For example, food banks and donation drives can help reduce hunger in local communities, leading to a healthier and more stable population. Furthermore, when citizens give their time and effort to support community projects, it creates a sense of unity and shared responsibility. As a result, communities become stronger and more resilient, as members feel they have a role in shaping their surroundings.
Commentary:

Topic Sentence: This paragraph transitions to societal benefits with a clear topic sentence.

Supporting Details: Concrete examples, such as food banks and donation drives, are provided to support the argument.

Explanation and Analysis: The societal effects of community service are analyzed, showing how collective action leads to stronger communities.

Body Paragraph 3: The Interconnectedness of Personal and Societal Benefits
It is important to note that the personal and societal benefits of community service are interconnected. As individuals grow through volunteer work, they become more engaged and empathetic citizens, which in turn leads to greater societal improvement. For instance, a student who volunteers in environmental clean-up efforts may develop a passion for sustainability, eventually influencing policies or initiatives that benefit the environment. In this way, community service acts as a cycle: personal development leads to greater social contribution, which in turn fosters more opportunities for personal growth.

Commentary:

Topic Sentence: This paragraph serves as a bridge, showing the connection between individual and societal benefits.

Supporting Details and Analysis: The example of environmental clean-up is used to illustrate how personal growth can lead to societal change. The analysis reinforces the thesis by showing how these two elements are interconnected.

Conclusion
In conclusion, community service provides valuable benefits for both individuals and society. On a personal level, it allows people to grow and develop important life skills. At the same time, it fosters stronger, more united communities. By volunteering, people not only improve themselves but also contribute to the well-being of society. It is clear that community service is a powerful force for good, creating a cycle of positive change that benefits everyone involved.

Commentary:

Restatement of Thesis: The conclusion restates the thesis, bringing the essay full circle.

Summary of Main Points: The personal and societal benefits are briefly summarized to remind the reader of the key arguments.

Closing Thought: The essay ends with a strong closing sentence that emphasizes the importance and power of community service, leaving the reader with something to think about.

Final Commentary on the Essay Writing Process:

Prewriting: Before writing, think about your topic and thesis. In this case, we decided to explore how community service benefits both individuals and society.

Drafting: Start with an introduction that presents your thesis clearly. In the body, use separate paragraphs to explore different aspects of your thesis, making sure each has its own topic sentence and supporting details.

Revising: Look for areas where you can improve clarity, coherence, or add stronger examples. Ensure that each paragraph logically connects to the next. Editing: Correct any grammar or punctuation errors, and make sure your wording is precise and formal.

Final Review: Read your essay one more time to check for flow and impact. This is an example of how to structure a well-organized essay, from introduction to conclusion, using evidence and clear analysis to support your thesis.

Example Essay 3

The Impact of Technology on Modern Education Introduction

Technology has revolutionized many aspects of our daily lives, and education is no exception. In modern classrooms, technology has transformed the way students learn, how teachers teach, and how educational content is delivered. From digital learning tools and virtual classrooms to online research and collaboration platforms, technology has made education more accessible, personalized, and engaging. In this essay, I will discuss the profound impact that technology has had on modern education, focusing on its ability to enhance learning experiences, increase access to education, and prepare students for a technology-driven world.

Commentary

Thesis Statement: The thesis clearly outlines the three main areas of focus—enhancing learning, increasing access, and preparing students for the future.
Hook/General Introduction: The opening sentence establishes the importance of technology in modern life, creating relevance for the topic. The introduction gives a general sense of how technology has reshaped education.

Body Paragraph 1: Enhancing Learning Experiences
One of the most significant ways technology has impacted modern education is by enhancing the learning experience for students. Digital tools such as interactive whiteboards, educational apps, and online simulations provide students with more engaging and dynamic learning environments. For instance, students studying biology can now participate in virtual dissections, allowing them to explore complex systems in a detailed, hands-on manner without the limitations of physical resources. Additionally, platforms like Khan Academy and Duolingo allow students to learn at their own pace, offering personalized learning experiences that cater to individual needs and learning styles. By making learning more interactive and adaptable, technology improves students' understanding and retention of information.

Commentary

Topic Sentence: The paragraph introduces the idea that technology enhances the learning experience, setting up a detailed discussion.

Supporting Details and Examples: Concrete examples such as virtual dissections and online learning platforms provide evidence to support the topic sentence.
Explanation and Analysis: The explanation connects the examples to the overall argument, showing how technology makes learning more interactive and effective.

Body Paragraph 2: Increasing Access to Education
Technology has also dramatically increased access to education, particularly for students who live in remote or underserved areas. With the rise of online courses, students can access high-quality education from anywhere in the world. Platforms such as Coursera, edX, and Google Classroom have made it possible for learners to participate in classes that were once only available at prestigious universities. Moreover, technology has made education more inclusive, with tools like speech-to-text software and screen readers enabling students with disabilities to participate more fully in the learning process. By breaking down geographic and physical barriers, technology has democratized education, making it more accessible to a broader range of students.

Commentary:

Topic Sentence: This paragraph shifts the focus to how technology increases access to education, with a clear and direct topic sentence.

Supporting Details: Specific examples of platforms and tools (Coursera, Google Classroom) are provided to illustrate how access has expanded.

Explanation and Analysis: The analysis explains how these technological advances have opened up educational opportunities for students who were previously excluded or limited by their circumstances. |

Body Paragraph 3: Preparing Students for a Technology-Driven World
In addition to enhancing learning and increasing access, technology plays a crucial role in preparing students for a future that is increasingly technology-driven. As automation and artificial intelligence continue to transform industries, students need to develop digital literacy and technical skills to succeed in the workforce. Schools and universities now integrate coding, robotics, and data science into their curriculums, ensuring that students are equipped with the tools they need to thrive in modern workplaces. Furthermore, collaborative platforms such as Google Drive and Microsoft Teams teach students how to work effectively in remote teams, a skill that is becoming essential in today's globalized job market. By incorporating technology into education, schools are preparing students to meet the demands of the future.

Commentary:

Topic Sentence: This paragraph focuses on how technology prepares students for the future, with a clear link to the essay's overall thesis.

Supporting Details and Examples: Examples of coding, robotics, and collaborative platforms are used to show how students are gaining practical skills for future careers.

Explanation and Analysis: The analysis connects these examples to the larger argument, demonstrating that technology is not just a tool for learning but also a preparation for real-world challenges.

Conclusion
In conclusion, the impact of technology on modern education is profound and far-reaching. It has enhanced the learning experience by making it more interactive and personalized, increased access to education by breaking down geographic and physical barriers, and prepared students for a future dominated by technological advancements. While technology poses some challenges, such as the need for digital equity, its overall effect on education has been overwhelmingly positive. As technology continues to evolve, so too will the possibilities for improving education, creating new opportunities for students and educators alike.

Commentary:

Restatement of Thesis: The conclusion reiterates the essay's main points, summarizing the benefits of technology in education.

Summary of Main Points: The personal and societal impacts of technology on education are restated to remind the reader of the key points discussed.

Closing Thought: The essay ends with a forward-looking statement about the continued evolution of technology and its potential to further improve education. This leaves the reader with a sense of ongoing progress.

Final Commentary on the Essay Writing Process:

Prewriting: Before beginning, we brainstormed the different ways technology impacts education, then developed a thesis that tied these ideas together.

Drafting: In the drafting stage, we organized our ideas into body paragraphs that each focused on one main point, supported by specific examples and analysis.

Revising: As we revised, we ensured that each paragraph was clear and flowed logically from one to the next, with transitions connecting the ideas.

Editing: We checked for any grammatical or structural issues, ensuring the essay is polished and easy to read.

Final Review: Finally, we gave the essay a thorough read to make sure the argument was cohesive, the evidence was strong, and the writing was engaging.
This essay demonstrates the importance of technology in modern education, structured with a clear thesis, supporting details, and thoughtful analysis throughout.

Example Essay Prompts

- Describe a person who has had a significant impact on your life and explain why.

- Discuss the importance of teamwork in achieving success.

- Analyze the effects of social media on relationships and communication.

- Explain how community service can benefit individuals and society as a whole.

- Compare and contrast two different cultures and discuss how they influence one another.

- Describe a challenge you have faced and how you overcame it.

- Discuss the impact of technology on modern education.

- Explain the benefits of reading for personal growth and development.

- Analyze the causes of climate change and propose potential solutions.

Common Essay Mistakes -Common Essay Mistakes - Example I

Whether the topic is love or action, reality television shows damage society. Viewers witness the personal struggles of strangers and they experience an outpouring of emotions in the name of entertainment. This can be dangerous on many levels. Viewers become numb to real emotions and values. Run the risk of not interpreting a dangerous situation correctly. 1 The reality show participant is also at risk because they are completely exposed. 2 The damage to both viewers and participants leads to the destruction of our healthy societal values.

Romance reality shows are dangerous to the participants and contribute to the emotional problems witnessed in society today as we set up a system built on equality and respect, shows like "The Bachelor" tear it down. 3 In front of millions of viewers every week, young women compete for a man. Twenty-five women claim to be in love with a man they just met. The man is reduced to an object they compete for. There are tears, fights, and manipulation aimed at winning the prize. 4 Imagine a young woman's reality when she returns home and faces the scrutiny of viewers who watched her unravel on television every Monday night. These women objectify themselves and have learned 5 that relationships are a combination of hysteria and competition. This does not give hope to a society based on family values and equality.

6 While incorporating the same manipulations and breakdown of relationships offered on "The Bachelor," shows like "Survivor" add another level of danger. Not only are they building a society based on lying to each other, they are competing in physical challenges that become dangerous. In the name of entertainment, these challenges become increasingly physical and are usually held in a hostile environment. The viewer's ability to determine the safety of an activity is messed up. 7 To entertain and preserve their pride, participants continue in competitions regardless of the danger level. For example, 8 participants on "Survivor" have sustained serious injuries as heart attack and burns. Societal rules are based on the safety of its citizens, not on hurting yourself for entertainment.

     Reality shows of all kinds are dangerous to participants. They damage society. 9

1. Correct sentence fragments. Who/what runs the risk? Add a subject or combine sentences. Try: "Viewers become numb to real emotions and run the risk of not interpreting a dangerous situation correctly."

2. Correct redundant phrases. Try: "The reality show participant is also at risk because they are exposed."

3. Correct run-on sentences. Decide which thoughts should be separated. Try: "Romance reality shows are dangerous to participants and contribute to the emotional problems of society today. As we support a system built on equality and respect, shows like "The Bachelor" tear it down."

4. Vary sentence structure and length. Try: "Twenty-five women claim to be in love with a man who is reduced to being the object of competition. There are tears, fights, and manipulation aimed at winning the prize."

5. Use active voice. Try: These women objectify themselves and learned that relationships are a combination of hysteria and competition.

6. Use transitions to tie paragraphs together. Try: Start the paragraph with, "Action oriented reality shows are equally as dangerous to the participants."

7. Avoid casual language/slang. Try: "The viewer's ability to determine the safety of an activity is compromised."

8. Don't address the essay. Avoid phrases like "for example" and "in conclusion." Try: "Participants on "Survivor" have sustained serious injuries in the form of heart attack and burns."

9. Leave yourself time to write a strong conclusion! Try: Designate 3-5 minutes for writing your conclusion.

Common Essay Mistakes - Example II

Questioning authority makes society stronger. In every aspect our society, there is an authoritative person or group making rules. There is also the group underneath them who are meant to follow. 1 This is true of our country's public schools as well as our federal government. The right to question authority at both of these levels is guaranteed by the United States Declaration of Independence. People are given the ability to question so that authority figures are kept in check 2 and will be forced to listen to the opinions of other people. Questioning authority leads to positive changes in society and preserves what is already working well.

If students never question the authority of a principal's decisions, the best interest of the student body is lost. Good things 3 may not remain in place for the students and no amendment to the rules are sought. Change requires that authority be questioned. An example of this is Silver Head Middle School in Davie, Florida. Last year, the principal felt strongly about enforcing the school's uniform policy. Some students were not bothered by this. 4 Many students felt the policy disregarded their civil rights. A petition voicing student dissatisfaction was signed and presented to the principal. He met with a student representative to discuss the petition. Compromise was reached in the form of a monthly "casual day." The students were able to promote change and peace by questioning authority.

Even at the level of federal government, our country's ultimate authority, the ability to question is the key to the harmony keeping society strong. Most government officials are elected by the public so they have the right to question their authority. 5 If there's a mandate, law, or statement that citizens aren't 6 happy with, they have recourse. Campaigning for, or against a political platform and participating in the electoral process give a voice to every opinion. I think elections are very important. 7 Without this questioning and examination of society's laws, the government will represent only the voice of the authority figure. The success of our society is based on the questioning of authority. 8

Society is strengthened by those who question authority. Dialogue is created between people with different visions and change becomes possible. At both the level of public school and of federal government, the positive effects of questioning authority can be witnessed. Whether questioning the decisions of a single principal or the motives of the federal government, it is the willingness of people to question and create change that allows society to grow. A strong society is inspired by many voices, all at different levels. 9 These voices keep society strong.

1. Write concisely. Combine the sentences to improve understanding and cut unnecessary words. Try: "In every aspect of society, there is an authority making rules and a group of people meant to follow them."

2. Avoid slang. Re-word "kept in check." Try: "People are given the ability to question so that authority figures are held accountable and will be forced to listen to the opinions of other people.

2-2. Cut unnecessary words. Try: "People are given the ability to question so that authority figures are held accountable and will listen to other opinions."

3. Use precise language. What are "good things?"Try: "Interesting activities may not remain in place for the students and no amendment to the rules are sought."

Use correct subject-verb agreement. Be careful to identify the correct subject of your sentence. Try: "Interesting activities may not remain in place for the students and no amendment to the rules is sought."

4. Don't add information that doesn't add value to your argument. Cut: "Some students weren't bothered by this."

5. Check for parallel structure. Who has the right to question whose authority? Try: "Having voted them in, the people have the authority to question public officials."

6. Don't use contractions in academic essays. Try: "If there is a mandate, law, or statement that citizens are not happy with, they have recourse."

7. Don't use the pronoun "I" in persuasive essays. Cut opinions. Cut: "I think elections are very important."

8. Use specific examples to prove your argument. Try: Discuss a particular election in depth.

9. Cut redundant sentences. Cut: "A strong society is inspired by many voices, all at different levels."

Writing Concisely

Concise writing is direct and descriptive. The reader follows the writer's thoughts easily. If your writing is concise, a four paragraph essay is acceptable for standardized tests. It's better to write clearly about fewer ideas than to write poorly about many.

This doesn't always mean using fewer words. It means that every word you use is important to the message. Unnecessary or repetitive information dilutes ideas and weakens your writing. The meaning of the word concise comes from the Latin, "to cut up." If it isn't necessary information, don't waste precious testing minutes writing it down.

Being redundant is a quick way to lengthen a sentence or paragraph, but it takes away your power during a timed essay. While many writers use repetition of phrases and key words to make their point, it's important to remove words that don't add value. Redundancy can confuse and lead you away from your subject when you need to write quickly. Be aware that many redundant phrases are part of our daily language and need to be cut from your essay.

For example, "bouquet of flowers" is a redundant phrase as only the word "bouquet" is necessary. Its definition includes flowers. Be especially careful with words you use to stress a point, such as "completely," "totally," and "very."

First of all, I'd like to thank my family.
Revised: First, I'd like to thank my family.

The school *introduced a new* rule.
Revised: The school introduced a rule.

I am *completely full*.
Revised: I am full.

Your glass is *totally empty*!
Revised: Your glass is empty!

Her artwork is *very unique*.
Revised: Her artwork is unique.

Other ways to cut bulk and time include avoiding phrases that have no meaning or power in your essay. Phrases like "in my opinion," "as a matter of fact," and "due to the fact that" are space and time wasters. Also, change passive verbs to active voice.

In my opinion, the paper is well written.
Revised: The paper is well written.

The book *was written* by the best students.
Revised: The best students wrote the book.

The teacher *is listening* to the students.
The teacher listens to the students.

This assigns action to the subject, shortens, and clarifies the sentence. When time is working against you, precise language is on your side.

Not only should you remove redundant phrases, whole sentences without value should be cut too. Replacing general nouns with specific ones is an effective way to accomplish this.

She screamed as the thing came closer. It was a sharp-toothed dog.
Revised: She screamed as the sharp-toothed dog came closer.

The revised sentence is precise and the paragraph is improved by combining sentences and varying sentence structure. When editing, ask yourself which thoughts should be connected and which need to be separated. Skim each paragraph as you finish writing it and cut as you go.

Leave three to four minutes for final editing. While reading, make a point to pause at every period. This allows you to "hear" sentences the way your reader will, not how you meant them to sound. This will help you find the phrases and sentences that need to be cut or combined.   The result is an essay a grader will appreciate.

PRACTICE TEST QUESTIONS SET 1

THE QUESTIONS BELOW ARE NOT THE SAME AS YOU WILL FIND ON THE ISEE® - THAT WOULD BE TOO EASY! And nobody knows what the questions will be and they change all the time. Below are general questions that cover the same subject areas as the ISEE®. So, while the format and exact wording of the questions may differ slightly, and change from year to year, if you can answer the questions below, you will have no problem with the ISEE®.

For the best results, take these practice test questions as if it were the real exam. Set aside time when you will not be disturbed, and a location that is quiet and free of distractions. Read the instructions carefully, read each question carefully, and answer to the best of your ability.

Use the bubble answer sheets provided. When you have completed the practice questions, check your answer against the Answer Key and read the explanation provided.

Do not attempt more than one set of practice test questions in one day. After completing the first practice test, wait two or three days before attempting the second set of questions.

Section I – Verbal Reasoning
Questions: 40 **Time:** 20 Minutes

Section II – Quantitative Reasoning
Questions: 35 **Time:** 35 Minutes

Section III – Reading
Questions: 40 **Time:** 40 Minutes

Section IV – Mathematics
Questions: 45 **Time:** 40 Minutes

Verbal Reasoning

	A	B	C	D	E		A	B	C	D	E
1	○	○	○	○	○	21	○	○	○	○	○
2	○	○	○	○	○	22	○	○	○	○	○
3	○	○	○	○	○	23	○	○	○	○	○
4	○	○	○	○	○	24	○	○	○	○	○
5	○	○	○	○	○	25	○	○	○	○	○
6	○	○	○	○	○	26	○	○	○	○	○
7	○	○	○	○	○	27	○	○	○	○	○
8	○	○	○	○	○	28	○	○	○	○	○
9	○	○	○	○	○	29	○	○	○	○	○
10	○	○	○	○	○	30	○	○	○	○	○
11	○	○	○	○	○	31	○	○	○	○	○
12	○	○	○	○	○	32	○	○	○	○	○
13	○	○	○	○	○	33	○	○	○	○	○
14	○	○	○	○	○	34	○	○	○	○	○

Quantitative Reasoning

1. Ⓐ Ⓑ Ⓒ Ⓓ
2. Ⓐ Ⓑ Ⓒ Ⓓ
3. Ⓐ Ⓑ Ⓒ Ⓓ
4. Ⓐ Ⓑ Ⓒ Ⓓ
5. Ⓐ Ⓑ Ⓒ Ⓓ
6. Ⓐ Ⓑ Ⓒ Ⓓ
7. Ⓐ Ⓑ Ⓒ Ⓓ
8. Ⓐ Ⓑ Ⓒ Ⓓ
9. Ⓐ Ⓑ Ⓒ Ⓓ
10. Ⓐ Ⓑ Ⓒ Ⓓ
11. Ⓐ Ⓑ Ⓒ Ⓓ
12. Ⓐ Ⓑ Ⓒ Ⓓ
13. Ⓐ Ⓑ Ⓒ Ⓓ
14. Ⓐ Ⓑ Ⓒ Ⓓ
15. Ⓐ Ⓑ Ⓒ Ⓓ
16. Ⓐ Ⓑ Ⓒ Ⓓ
17. Ⓐ Ⓑ Ⓒ Ⓓ

18. Ⓐ Ⓑ Ⓒ Ⓓ
19. Ⓐ Ⓑ Ⓒ Ⓓ
20. Ⓐ Ⓑ Ⓒ Ⓓ
21. Ⓐ Ⓑ Ⓒ Ⓓ
22. Ⓐ Ⓑ Ⓒ Ⓓ
23. Ⓐ Ⓑ Ⓒ Ⓓ
24. Ⓐ Ⓑ Ⓒ Ⓓ
25. Ⓐ Ⓑ Ⓒ Ⓓ
26. Ⓐ Ⓑ Ⓒ Ⓓ
27. Ⓐ Ⓑ Ⓒ Ⓓ
28. Ⓐ Ⓑ Ⓒ Ⓓ
29. Ⓐ Ⓑ Ⓒ Ⓓ
30. Ⓐ Ⓑ Ⓒ Ⓓ
31. Ⓐ Ⓑ Ⓒ Ⓓ
32. Ⓐ Ⓑ Ⓒ Ⓓ
33. Ⓐ Ⓑ Ⓒ Ⓓ
34. Ⓐ Ⓑ Ⓒ Ⓓ

35. Ⓐ Ⓑ Ⓒ Ⓓ

Reading

	A	B	C	D	E		A	B	C	D	E
1	○	○	○	○	○	21	○	○	○	○	○
2	○	○	○	○	○	22	○	○	○	○	○
3	○	○	○	○	○	23	○	○	○	○	○
4	○	○	○	○	○	24	○	○	○	○	○
5	○	○	○	○	○	25	○	○	○	○	○
6	○	○	○	○	○	26	○	○	○	○	○
7	○	○	○	○	○	27	○	○	○	○	○
8	○	○	○	○	○	28	○	○	○	○	○
9	○	○	○	○	○	29	○	○	○	○	○
10	○	○	○	○	○	30	○	○	○	○	○
11	○	○	○	○	○	31	○	○	○	○	○
12	○	○	○	○	○	32	○	○	○	○	○
13	○	○	○	○	○	33	○	○	○	○	○
14	○	○	○	○	○	34	○	○	○	○	○
15	○	○	○	○	○	35	○	○	○	○	○
16	○	○	○	○	○	36	○	○	○	○	○
17	○	○	○	○	○	37	○	○	○	○	○
18	○	○	○	○	○	38	○	○	○	○	○
19	○	○	○	○	○	39	○	○	○	○	○
20	○	○	○	○	○	40	○	○	○	○	○

Mathematics

1. A B C D
2. A B C D
3. A B C D
4. A B C D
5. A B C D
6. A B C D
7. A B C D
8. A B C D
9. A B C D
10. A B C D
11. A B C D
12. A B C D
13. A B C D
14. A B C D
15. A B C D
16. A B C D
17. A B C D
18. A B C D
19. A B C D
20. A B C D
21. A B C D
22. A B C D
23. A B C D
24. A B C D
25. A B C D
26. A B C D
27. A B C D
28. A B C D
29. A B C D
30. A B C D
31. A B C D
32. A B C D
33. A B C D
34. A B C D
35. A B C D
36. A B C D
37. A B C D
38. A B C D
39. A B C D
40. A B C D
41. A B C D
42. A B C D
43. A B C D
44. A B C D
45. A B C D

Part I – Synonyms

Directions: Choose the word that is closest in meaning to the given word.

1. **PECULIAR**
    a. New
    b. Strange
    c. Imaginative
    d. Funny

2. **TIPPET**
    a. Necktie
    b. Shawl
    c. Sweater
    d. Blouse

3. **VIVID**
    a. Glamorous
    b. Bountiful
    c. Varied
    d. Brilliant

4. **SEMBLANCE**
    a. Personality
    b. Image
    c. Attitude
    d. ambition

5. **IMPREGNABLE**
    a. Unconquerable
    b. Impossible
    c. Unlimited
    d. Imperfect

6. **JARGON**
    a. Slang
    b. Slander
    c. Plagiarism
    d. Outdated

7. **RENDER**
    a. Give
    b. Recognize
    c. Stem
    d. Adjust

8. **INTRUSIVE**
    a. Private
    b. Invasive
    c. Mysterious
    d. Unique

9. **RENOWN**
    a. Popular
    b. Safe
    c. Shy
    d. Curtail

10. **INCOHERENT**
    a. Ambiguous
    b. Lighthearted
    c. Jumbled
    d. Malignant

11. **CONGENIAL**
    a. Pleasant
    b. Distort
    c. Valuable
    d. Liability

12. PLIGHT

a. Circumstance
b. Scheme
c. Whimsical
d. Situation

13. BERATE

a. Criticize
b. Unspoken
c. Tenet
d. Turf

14. CONSTRUE

a. Decide
b. Design
c. Interpret
d. Examine

15. SCARED

a. Surprised
b. Grateful
c. Happy
d. Terrified

16. DEMONSTRATED

a. Presented
b. Exclaimed
c. Handled
d. Lectured

17. HALT

a. Continue
b. Start
c. Stop
d. Danger

18. STRANGE

a. Popular
b. Ordinary
c. Unfamiliar
d. Common

19. SEIZE

a. Lose
b. Choose
c. Rob
d. Win

20. DIVULGE

a. Repeat
b. Tell
c. Write
d. Imagine

Part II - Sentence Completion

Directions: For each sentence below, choose the word that best completes the sentence.

21. Through the use of powerful fans that circulate the heat over the food, _____ ovens work very efficiently.

    a. Microwave
    b. Broiler
    c. Convection
    d. Pressure

22. Because of the growing use of _____ as a fuel, corn production has greatly increased.

    a. Alcohol
    b. Ethanol
    c. Natural gas
    d. Oil

23. In heavily industrialized areas, the air pollution causes many _____ diseases.

    a. Respiratory
    b. Cardiac
    c. Alimentary
    d. Circulatory

24. Because hydroelectric power is a _____ source of energy, its use is considered a green energy.

    a. Significant
    b. Disposable
    c. Renewable
    d. Recyclable

25. The process required the use of highly _____ liquids, so fire extinguishers were everywhere in the factory.

    a. Erratic
    b. Combustible
    c. Inflammable
    d. Neutral

26. I still don't know exactly. That isn't _____ evidence.

    a. Undeterred
    b. Unrelenting
    c. Unfortunate
    d. Conclusive

27. He could manipulate the coins in his fingers very _____.

    a. Brazenly
    b. Eloquently
    c. Boisterously
    d. Deftly

28. His investment scheme _____ many serious investors, who lost money.

    a. Helped
    b. Vindicated
    c. Duped
    d. Reproved

29. When we go to a party, we always _____ a driver.

    a. Feign
    b. Exploit
    c. Dote
    d. Designate

30. This new evidence should _____ any doubts.

   a. Dispel
   b. Dispense
   c. Evaluate
   d. Diverse

31. She went to Asia on $10 a day – her _____ travelling plans are amazing.

   a. Frothy
   b. Frugal
   c. Fraught
   d. Focal

32. My grandmother's house is full or trinkets and ornaments. She is always buying _____.

   a. Collectibles
   b. Baubles
   c. China
   d. Crystal

33. I am finally out of debt! I paid off all of my _____.

   a. Debtors
   b. Defendants
   c. Accounts Receivable
   d. Creditors

34. I love listening to his speeches. He has a gift for _____.

   a. Oratory
   b. Irony
   c. Jargon
   d. None of the above

35. The warehouse went bankrupt so all of the furniture has to be _____.

   a. Dissected
   b. Liquidated
   c. Destroyed
   d. Bought

36. He sold the property when he didn't even own it. The whole thing was a _____.

   a. Hoax
   b. Feign
   c. Defile
   d. Default

37. The repair really isn't working. Those parts you replaced are _____.

   a. Despondent
   b. Illusive
   c. Defective'
   d. Granular

38. Just because she is supervisor, doesn't mean we have to _____ in front of her.

   a. Foible
   b. Grovel
   c. Humiliate
   d. Indispose

39. That noise is _____ ! It is driving me crazy.

   a. Loud
   b. Intolerable
   c. Frivolous
   d. Fictitious

40. Her inheritance was a good size and included many _____.

   a. Heirlooms
   b. Perchance
   c. Cynical
   d. Lateral

Section II – Quantitative Reasoning

1. Solve for x. 5x + 21 = 66.

   a. 19
   b. 9
   c. 15
   d. 5

2. What is the least common multiple of 9 and 3?

   a. 27
   b. 9
   c. 3
   d. 18

3. How much water can be stored in a cylindrical container 5 meters in diameter and 12 meters high?

   a. 235.65 m³
   b. 223.65 m³
   c. 240.65 m³
   d. 252.65 m³

4. Estimate 215 x 65.

   a. 1,350
   b. 13,500
   c. 103,500
   d. 3,500

5. Richard gives 's' amount of salary to each of his 'n' employees weekly. If he has 'x' amount of money then how many days he can employ these 'n' employees.

   a. sx/7n
   b. 7x
   c. nx/7x
   d. 7x/ns

6. Below is the attendance for a class of 45.

   Day   Absent Students
   Monday   5
   Tuesday   9
   Wednesday 4
   Thursday   10
   Friday   6

   What is the average attendance for the week?

   a. 88%
   b. 85%
   c. 81%
   d. 77%

7. A driver at a speed of 's' miles per hour can reach his destination in 'h' hours. If his speed increased from 's' to 'x' then how much less time in hours will it take to reach his destination?

   a. h – xh/s
   b. h - sh/x
   c. s/x
   d. sh/x

8. Write 41.061 to the nearest 10th.

   a. 41.1
   b. 41.06
   c. 41
   d. 41.6

9. Brad has agreed to buy everyone a Coke. Each drink costs $1.89, and there are 5 friends. Estimate Brad's cost.

   a. $7
   b. $8
   c. $10
   d. $12

10. In a train one morning, 24 people are sitting while 8 people are standing. What is the ratio of people sitting to standing?

    a. 1:3
    b. 1:5
    c. 3:1
    d. 3:5

11. Estimate 4,210,987 – 210,078

    a. 4,000,000
    b. 40,000,000
    c. 400,000
    d. 40,000

12. 2^3 =

    a. 1/0.125
    b. $\sqrt{16}$
    c. 3^2
    d. 5

13. 10^4 is not equal to which of the following?

    a. 100,000
    b. 0.1×10^5
    c. $10 \times 10 \times 10 \times 10$
    d. $10^2 \times 10^2$

14. Divide x^5 by x^2

    a. x^7
    b. x^4
    c. x^{10}
    d. x^3

15. Which of the following is not a fraction equivalent to 3/4?

    a. 6/8
    b. 9/12
    c. 12/18
    d. 21/28

16. Which of the following numbers is the greatest?

    a. 1
    b. $\sqrt{2}$
    c. 3/2
    d. 4/3

17. What number divided by 5 is 1/4 of 100?

    a. 125
    b. 150
    c. 75
    d. 225

Part II

Directions: Examine the quantities given in Column A and Column B of the table and choose the best answer.

18.

Column A	Column B
20 - X	X^2

$3X + 3 = 15$

    a. Column A is greater
    b. Column B is greater
    c. The quantities are equal
    d. The relationship cannot be determined

19.

Column A	Column B
2X + Y	2Y + X

$X > 0, Y > 0$

    a. Column A is greater
    b. Column B is greater
    c. The quantities are equal
    d. The relationship cannot be determined

20.

Column A	Column B
3	Y

$y^2 + 6 = 15$

    a. Column A is greater
    b. Column B is greater
    c. The quantities are equal
    d. The relationship cannot be determined

21.

Column A	Column B
A	14

$2ab + 5 = 25$

    a. Column A is greater
    b. Column B is greater
    c. The quantities are equal
    d. The relationship cannot be determined

22.

Column A	Column B
1/2	0.589/.35

    a. Column A is greater
    b. Column B is greater
    c. The quantities are equal
    d. The relationship cannot be determined

23.

Column A	Column B
2/3	0.589/.35

    a. Column A is greater
    b. Column B is greater
    c. The quantities are equal
    d. The relationship cannot be determined

24.

Column A	Column B
4/9 + 3/4	24/27

a. Column A is greater

b. Column B is greater

c. The quantities are equal

d. The relationship cannot be determined

25.

Column A	Column B
Susan's Savings	$75

Susan bought a dishwasher on sale for 20% off. She has a membership that gives her an additional 2% off the sale price. The full retail price of the dishwasher was $250.

a. Column A is greater

b. Column B is greater

c. The quantities are equal

d. The relationship cannot be determined

26.

Column A	Column B
3.1 hours	X hours

A car drove 135 km. at a speed of 50 km. per hour. Let X equal the time it took.

a. Column A is greater

b. Column B is greater

c. The quantities are equal

d. The relationship cannot be determined

27.

Column A	Column B
X pages	40 pages

A typist can type a full page in 2 minutes. Let X be the number of pages he can type in 1 hour.

a. Column A is greater

b. Column B is greater

c. The quantities are equal

d. The relationship cannot be determined

28.

Column A	Column B
X	$10.15

Jack bought 2 cheeseburgers for $3.00 each, a large fries for $1.99 and a Coke for $1.58. A tax of 3.2% was added. If he paid with a $20 bill, let X be the amount of change he received.

a. Column A is greater

b. Column B is greater

c. The quantities are equal

d. The relationship cannot be determined

29.

Column A	Column B
X	$645,730

A business owner has assets as follows:

Building: $580,000
Machinery: $255,000
Cash: $10,000

At the end of one year, the building has increased by 5.6%, the machinery has depreciated by 15% and he has $4500 in additional cash.

   a. Column A is greater
   b. Column B is greater
   c. The quantities are equal
   d. The relationship cannot be determined

30.

Column A	Column B
X	$40

Britney invested $500 in a fixed-term deposit for 2 years. Interest of 4% was paid yearly. Let X be the amount of interest she earned.

   a. Column A is greater
   b. Column B is greater
   c. The quantities are equal
   d. The relationship cannot be determined

31.

Column A	Column B
Average number of students absent	4

Below is the number of students absent for 1 week.

Monday: 5
Tuesday 8
Wednesday 2
Thursday 0
Friday 4

   a. Column A is greater
   b. Column B is greater
   c. The quantities are equal
   d. The relationship cannot be determined

32.

Column A	Column B
3/4 expressed as percent	80%

   a. Column A is greater
   b. Column B is greater
   c. The quantities are equal
   d. The relationship cannot be determined

33.

Column A	Column B
.78 as a fraction	8/10

   a. Column A is greater
   b. Column B is greater
   c. The quantities are equal
   d. The relationship cannot be determined

34.

Column A	Column B
65%	5/6

   a. Column A is greater
   b. Column B is greater
   c. The quantities are equal
   d. The relationship cannot be determined

35.

Column A	Column B
.27	25% of .8

   a. Column A is greater
   b. Column B is greater
   c. The quantities are equal
   d. The relationship cannot be determined

Section III - Reading

Questions 1 – 4 refer to the following passage.

Passage 1 When a Poet Longs to Mourn, He Writes an Elegy

Poems are an expressive, especially emotional, form of writing. They have been present in literature virtually from the time civilizations invented the written word. Poets often portrayed as moody, secluded, and even troubled, but this is because poets are introspective and feel deeply about the current events and cultural norms they are surrounded with. Poets often produce the most telling literature, giving insight into the society and mind-set they come from. This can be done in many forms.

The oldest types of poems often include many stanzas, may or may not rhyme, and are more about telling a story than experimenting with language or words. The most common types of ancient poetry are epics, which are usually extremely long stories that follow a hero through his journey, or elegies, which are often solemn in tone and used to mourn or lament something or someone. The Mesopotamians are often said to have invented the written word, and their literature is among the oldest in the world, including the epic poem titled "Epic of Gilgamesh." Similar in style and length to "Gilgamesh" is "Beowulf," an elegy poem written in Old English and set in Scandinavia. These poems are often used by professors as the earliest examples of literature.

The importance of poetry was revived in the Renaissance. At this time, Europeans discovered the style and beauty of ancient Greek arts, and poetry was among those. Shakespeare is the most well-known poet of the time, and he used poetry not only to write poems but also to write plays for the theater. The most popular forms of poetry during the Renaissance included villanelles, sonnets, as well as the epic. Poets during this time focused on style and form, and developed very specific rules and outlines for how an exceptional poem should be written.

As often happens in the arts, modern poets have rejected the constricting rules of Renaissance poets, and free form poems are much more popular. Some modern poems would read just like stories if they weren't arranged into lines and stanzas. It is difficult to tell which poems and poets will be the most important, because works of art often become more famous in hindsight, after the poet has died and society can look at itself without being in the moment. Modern poetry continues to develop, and will no doubt continue to change as values, thought, and writing continue to change.

Poems can be among the most enlightening and uplifting texts for a person to read if they are looking to connect with the past, connect with other people, or try to gain an understanding of what is happening in their time.

1. In summary, the author has written this passage

    a. as a foreword that will introduce a poem in a book or magazine.

    b. because she loves poetry and wants more people to like it.

    c. to give a brief history of poems.

    d. in order to convince students to write poems.

2. The author organizes the paragraphs mainly by

    a. moving chronologically, explaining which types of poetry were common in that time.

    b. talking about new types of poems each paragraph and explaining them a little.

    c. focusing on one poet or group of people and the poems they wrote.

    d. explaining older types of poetry so she can talk about modern poetry.

3. The author's claim that poetry has been around "virtually from the time civilizations invented the written word" is supported by the detail that

    a. Beowulf is written in Old English, which is not really in use any longer.

    b. epic poems told stories about heroes.

    c. the Renaissance poets tried to copy Greek poets.

    d. the Mesopotamians are credited with both inventing the word and writing "Epic of Gilgamesh."

4. According to the passage, it can be understood that the word "telling" means

    a. speaking.

    b. significant.

    c. soothing.

    d. wordy.

Questions 5 – 8 refer to the following passage.

Passage 2 - Viruse

A virus (from the Latin virus meaning toxin or poison) is a small infectious agent that can replicate only inside the living cells of other organisms. Most viruses are too small to be seen directly with a microscope. Viruses infect all types of organisms, from animals and plants to bacteria and single-celled organisms.

Unlike prions and viroids, viruses consist of two or three parts: all viruses have genes made from either DNA or RNA, all have a protein coat that protects these genes, and some have an envelope of fat that surrounds them when they are outside a cell. (Viroids do not have a protein coat and prions contain no RNA or DNA.) Viruses vary from simple to very complex structures. Most viruses are about one hundred times smaller than an average bacterium. The origins of viruses in the evolutionary history of life are unclear: some may have evolved from plasmids—pieces of DNA that can move between cells—while others may have evolved from bacteria.

Viruses spread in many ways; plant viruses are often transmitted from plant to plant by insects that feed on sap, such as aphids, while animal viruses can be carried by blood-sucking insects. These disease-bearing organisms are known as vectors. Influenza viruses are spread by coughing and sneezing. HIV is one of several viruses transmitted through sexual contact and by exposure to infected blood. Viruses can infect only a limited range of host cells called the "host range." This can be broad as when a virus is capable of infecting many species or narrow.

https://en.wikipedia.org/wiki/Virus.

5. What can we infer from the first paragraph in this selection?

    a. A virus is the same as bacterium.
    b. A person with excellent vision can see a virus with the naked eye.
    c. A virus cannot be seen with the naked eye.
    d. Not all viruses are dangerous.

6. What types of organisms do viruses infect?

    a. Only plants and humans
    b. Only animals and humans
    c. Only disease-prone humans
    d. All types of organisms

7. How many parts do prions and viroids consist of?

a. Two
b. Three
c. Either less than two or more than three
d. Less than two

8. What is one common virus spread by coughing and sneezing?

a. AIDS
b. Influenza
c. Herpes
d. Tuberculosis

Questions 9 – 11 refer to the following passage.

Passage 3 – The Life of Helen Keller

Many people have heard of Helen Keller. She is famous because she was unable to see or hear, but learned to speak and read and went onto attend college and earn a degree. Her life is a very interesting story, one that she developed into an autobiography, which was then adapted into both a stage play and a movie. How did Helen Keller overcome her disabilities to become a famous woman? Read on to find out.

Helen Keller was not born blind and deaf. When she was a small baby, she had a very high fever for several days. As a result of her sudden illness, baby Helen lost her eyesight and her hearing. Because she was so young when she went deaf and blind, Helen Keller never had any recollection of being able to see or hear. Since she could not hear, she could not learn to talk. Since she could not see, it was difficult for her to move around. For the first six years of her life, her world was very still and dark.

Imagine what Helen's childhood was like. She could not hear her mother's voice. She could not see the beauty of her parent's farm. She could not recognize who was giving her a hug, or a bath or even where her bedroom was each night. Sadly, she could not communicate with her parents in any way. She could not express her feelings or tell them the things she wanted. It must have been a very sad childhood.

When Helen was six years old, her parents hired her a teacher named Anne Sullivan. Anne was a young woman who was almost blind. However, she could hear and she could read Braille, so she was a perfect teacher for young Helen. At first, Anne had a very hard time teaching Helen anything. She described her first impression of Helen as a "wild thing, not a child." Helen did not like Anne at first either. She bit and hit Anne when Anne tried to teach her. However, the two of them eventually came to have a great deal of love and respect.

Anne taught Helen to hear by putting her hands on people's throats. She could feel the sounds people made. In time, Helen learned to feel what people said. Next, Anne taught Helen to read Braille, which is how books are written for the blind. Finally, Anne taught Helen to talk. Although Helen did learn to talk, it was hard for anyone but Anne to understand her.

As Helen grew older, she amazed more and more people with her story. She went to college and wrote books about her life. She gave talks to the public, with Anne at her side, translating her words. Today, both Anne Sullivan and Helen Keller are famous women who are respected for their lives' work.

9. Helen Keller could not see and hear and so, what was her biggest problem in childhood?

    a. Inability to communicate

    b. Inability to walk

    c. Inability to play

    d. Inability to eat

10. Helen learned to hear by feeling the vibrations people made when they spoke. What were these vibrations were felt through?

    a. Mouth

    b. Throat

    c. Ears

    d. Lips

11. From the passage, we can infer that Anne Sullivan was a patient teacher. We can infer this because

    a. Helen hit and bit her and Anne remained her teacher.

    b. Anne taught Helen to read only.

    c. Anne was hard of hearing too.

    d. Anne wanted to be a teacher.

Questions 12 – 14 refer to the following passage.

Passage 4 – US Weather Service

The United States National Weather Service classifies thunderstorms as severe when they reach a predetermined level. Usually, this means the storm is strong enough to inflict wind or hail damage. In most of the United States, a storm is considered severe if winds reach over 50 knots (58 mph or 93 km/h), hail is ¾ inch (2 cm) diameter or larger, or if meteorologists report funnel clouds or tornadoes. In the Central Region of the United States National Weather Service, the hail threshold for a severe thunderstorm is 1 inch (2.5 cm) in diameter. Though a funnel cloud or tornado indicates the presence of a severe thunderstorm, the various meteorological agencies would issue a tornado warning rather than a severe thunderstorm warning here.

Meteorologists in Canada define a severe thunderstorm as either having tornadoes, wind gusts of 90 km/h or greater, hail 2 centimeters in diameter or greater, rainfall more than 50 millimeters in 1 hour, or 75 millimeters in 3 hours.

Severe thunderstorms can develop from any type of thunderstorm.

http://en.wikipedia.org/wiki/Outline_of_meteorology.

12. What is the purpose of this passage?

   a. Explaining when a thunderstorm turns into a tornado.

   b. Explaining who issues storm warnings, and when these warnings should be issued.

   c. Explaining when meteorologists consider a thunderstorm severe.

   d. None of the above.

13. It is possible to infer from this passage that

   a. Different areas and countries have different criteria for determining a severe storm.

   b. Thunderstorms can include lightning and tornadoes, as well as violent winds and large hail.

   c. If someone spots both a thunderstorm and a tornado, meteorological agencies will immediately issue a severe storm warning.

   d. Canada has a much different alert system for severe storms, with criteria that are far less.

14. What would the Central Region of the United States National Weather Service do if hail was 2.7 cm in diameter?

   a. Not issue a severe thunderstorm warning.

   b. Issue a tornado warning.

   c. Issue a severe thunderstorm warning.

   d. Sleet must also accompany the hail before the Weather Service will issue a storm warning.

Questions 15 – 18 refer to the following passage.

Passage 5 – Low Blood Sugar

As the name suggest, low blood sugar is low sugar levels in the bloodstream. This can occur when you have not eaten properly and undertake strenuous activity, or, when you are very hungry. When Low blood sugar occurs regularly and is ongoing, it is a medical condition called hypoglycemia. This condition can occur in diabetics and in healthy adults.

Causes of low blood sugar can include excessive alcohol consumption, metabolic problems, stomach surgery, pancreas, liver or kidneys problems, as well as a side-effect of some medications.

Symptoms

There are different symptoms depending on the severity of the case.

Mild hypoglycemia can lead to feelings of nausea and hunger. The patient may also feel nervous, jittery and have fast heart beats. Sweaty skin, clammy and cold skin are likely symptoms.
Moderate hypoglycemia can result in a short temper, confusion, nervousness, fear and blurring of vision. The patient may feel weak and unsteady.

Severe cases of hypoglycemia can lead to seizures, coma, fainting spells, nightmares, headaches, excessive sweats and severe tiredness.

Diagnosis of low blood sugar

A doctor can diagnosis this medical condition by asking the patient questions and testing blood and urine samples. Home testing kits are available for patients to monitor blood sugar levels. It is important to see a qualified doctor though. The doctor can administer tests to ensure that will safely rule out other medical conditions that could affect blood sugar levels.

Treatment

Quick treatments include drinking or eating foods and drinks with high sugar contents. Good examples include soda, fruit juice, hard candy and raisins. Glucose energy tablets can also help. Doctors may also recommend medications and well as changes in diet and exercise routine to treat chronic low blood sugar.

15. Based on the article, which of the following is true?

    a. Low blood sugar can happen to anyone.

    b. Low blood sugar only happens to diabetics.

    c. Low blood sugar can occur even.

    d. None of the statements are true.

16. Which of the following are the author's opinion?

   a. Quick treatments include drinking or eating foods and drinks with high sugar contents.

   b. None of the statements are opinions.

   c. This condition can occur in diabetics and in healthy adults.

   d. There are different symptoms depending on the severity of the case

17. What is the author's purpose?

   a. To inform

   b. To persuade

   c. To entertain

   d. To analyze

18. Which of the following is not a detail?

   a. A doctor can diagnosis this medical condition by asking the patient questions and testing.

   b. A doctor will test blood and urine samples.

   c. Glucose energy tablets can also help.

   d. Home test kits monitor blood sugar levels.

   d. None of the above.

Questions 19 - 22 refer to the following recipe.

Chocolate Chip Cookies

3/4 cup sugar
3/4 cup packed brown sugar
1 cup butter, softened
2 large eggs, beaten
1 teaspoon vanilla extract
2 1/4 cups all-purpose flour
1 teaspoon baking soda
3/4 teaspoon salt
2 cups semisweet chocolate chips
If desired, 1 cup chopped pecans, or chopped walnuts.
Preheat oven to 375 degrees.

Mix sugar, brown sugar, butter, vanilla and eggs in a large bowl. Stir in flour, baking soda, and salt. The dough will be very stiff.

Stir in chocolate chips by hand with a sturdy wooden spoon. Add the pecans, or other nuts, if desired. Stir until the chocolate chips and nuts are evenly dispersed.

Drop dough by rounded tablespoonfuls 2 inches apart onto a cookie sheet.

Bake 8 to 10 minutes or until light brown. Cookies may look underdone, but they will finish cooking after you take them out of the oven.

19. What is the correct order for adding these ingredients?

    a. Brown sugar, baking soda, chocolate chips
    b. Baking soda, brown sugar, chocolate chips
    c. Chocolate chips, baking soda, brown sugar
    d. Baking soda, chocolate chips, brown sugar

20. What does sturdy mean?

    a. Long
    b. Strong
    c. Short
    d. Wide

21. What does disperse mean?

    a. Scatter
    b. To form a ball
    c. To stir
    d. To beat

22. When can you stop stirring the nuts?

    a. When the cookies are cooked
    b. When the nuts are evenly distributed
    c. As soon as the nuts are added
    d. After the chocolate chips are added

Questions 23 – 26 refer to the following passage.

Passage 7 - Ways Characters Communicate in Theater

Playwrights give their characters voices in a way that gives depth and added meaning to what happens on stage during their play. There are different types of speech in scripts that allow characters to talk with themselves, with other characters, and even with the audience.

It is very unique to theater that characters may talk "to themselves." When characters do this, the speech they give is called a soliloquy. Soliloquies are usually poetic, introspective, moving, and can tell audience members about the feelings, motivations, or suspicions of an individual character without that character having to reveal them to other characters on stage. "To be or not to be" is a famous soliloquy given by Hamlet as he considers difficult but important themes, such as life and death.

The most common type of communication in plays is when one character is speaking to another or a group of other characters. This is generally called dialogue, but can also be called monologue if one character speaks without being interrupted for a long time. It is not necessarily the most important type of communication, but it is the most common because the plot of the play cannot really progress without it.

Lastly, and most unique to theater (although it has been used somewhat in film) is when a character speaks directly to the audience. This is called an aside, and scripts usually specifically direct actors to do this. Asides are usually comical, an inside joke between the character and the audience, and very short. The actor will usually face the audience when delivering them, even if it's for a moment, so the audience can recognize this move as an aside.
All three of these types of communication are important to the art of theater, and have been perfected by famous playwrights like Shakespeare. Understanding these types of communication can help an audience member grasp what is artful about the script and action of a play.

23. According to the passage, characters in plays communicate to

    a. move the plot forward.
    b. show the private thoughts and feelings of one character.
    c. make the audience laugh.
    d. add beauty and artistry to the play.

24. When Hamlet delivers "To be or not to be," he can most likely be described as

a. solitary.

b. thoughtful.

c. dramatic.

d. hopeless.

25. The author uses parentheses to punctuate "although it has been used somewhat in film,"

a. to show that films are less important.

b. instead of using commas so that the sentence is not interrupted.

c. because parenthesis help separate details that are not as important.

d. to show that films are not as artistic.

26. It can be understood that by the phrase "give their characters voices," the author means that

a. playwrights are generous.

b. playwrights are changing the sound or meaning of characters' voices to fit what they had in mind.

c. dialogue is important in creating characters.

d. playwrights may be the parent of one of their actors and literally give them their voice.

Questions 27 – 30 refer to the following passage.

Passage 8 – Navy SEAL

The United States Navy's Sea, Air and Land Teams, commonly known as Navy SEALs, are the U.S. Navy's principle special operations force, and a part of the Naval Special Warfare Command (NSWC) as well as the maritime component of the United States Special Operations Command (USSOCOM).

The unit's acronym ("SEAL") comes from their capacity to operate at sea, in the air, and on land – but it is their ability to work underwater that separates SEALs from most other military units in the world. Navy SEALs are trained and have been deployed in a wide variety of missions, including direct action and special reconnaissance operations, unconventional warfare, foreign internal defence, hostage rescue, counter-terrorism and other missions. All SEALs are members of either the United States Navy or the United States Coast Guard.

In the early morning of May 2, 2011 local time, a team of 40 CIA-led Navy SEALs completed an operation to kill Osama bin Laden in Abbottabad, Pakistan about 35 miles (56 km) from Islamabad, the country's capital. The Navy SEALs were part of the Naval Special Warfare Development Group, previously called "Team 6." President Barack Obama later confirmed the death of bin Laden. The unprecedented media coverage raised the public profile of the SEAL community, particularly the counter-terrorism specialists commonly known as SEAL Team 6.

https://en.wikipedia.org/wiki/United_States_Navy_SEALs.

27. Are Navy SEALs part of USSOCOM?

   a. Yes
   b. No
   c. Only for special operations
   d. No, they are part of the US Navy

28. What separates Navy SEALs from other military units?

   a. Belonging to NSWC
   b. Direct action and special reconnaissance operations
   c. Working underwater
   d. Working for other military units in the world

29. What other military organizations do SEALs belong to?

   a. The US Navy
   b. The Coast Guard
   c. The US Army
   d. The Navy and the Coast Guard

30. What other organization participated in the Bin Laden raid?

   a. The CIA
   b. The US Military
   c. Counter-terrorism specialists
   d. None of the above

Questions 31 – 34 refer to the following passage.

Passage 9 - How To Get A Good Nights Sleep

Sleep is just as essential for healthy living as water, air and food. Sleep allows the body to rest and replenish depleted energy levels. Sometimes we may for various reasons have trouble sleeping which has a serious effect on our health. Those who have prolonged sleeping problems are facing a serious medical condition and should see a qualified doctor when possible for help. Here is simple guide that can help you sleep better at night.

Try to create a natural pattern of waking up and sleeping around the same time every day. This means avoiding going to bed too early and oversleeping past your usual wake up time. Going to bed and getting up at radically different times everyday confuses your body clock. Try to establish a natural rhythm as much as you can.

Exercises and a bit of physical activity can help you sleep better at night. If you are having problem sleeping, try to be as active as you can during the day. If you are tired from physical activity, falling asleep is a natural and easy process
for your body. If you remain inactive during the day, you will find it harder to sleep properly at night. Try walking, jogging, swimming or simple stretches close to your bed time.

Afternoon naps are great to refresh you during the day, but they may also keep you awake at night. If you feel sleepy during the day, get up, take a walk and get busy to keep from sleeping. Stretching is a good way to increase blood flow to the brain and keep you alert so that you don't sleep during the day. This will help you sleep better night.

> A warm bath or a glass of milk in the evening can help your body relax and prepare for sleep. A cold bath will wake you up and keep you up for several hours. Also avoid eating too late before bed.

31. How would you describe this sentence?

　a. A recommendation
　b. An opinion
　c. A fact
　d. A diagnosis

32. Which of the following is an alternative title for this article?

a. Exercise and a good night's sleep
b. Benefits of a good night's sleep
c. Tips for a good night's sleep
d. Lack of sleep is a serious medical condition

33. Which of the following cannot be inferred from this article?

a. Biking is helpful for getting a good night's sleep
b. Mental activity is helpful for getting a good night's sleep
c. Eating bedtime snacks is not recommended
d. Getting up at the same time is helpful for a good night's sleep

34. What is a disadvantage of taking naps?

a. They may keep you awake.
b. There are no disadvantages
c. They may help you sleep better
d. They may affect your diet

Questions 35 – 36 refer to the following passage.

Passage 10 - Gardens

Ancient Roman gardens are known for their statues and sculptures, which were never missing from the lives of Romans. Romans designed their gardens with hedges and vines as well as a wide variety of flowers, including acanthus, cornflowers and crocus, cyclamen, hyacinth, iris and ivy, lavender, lilies, myrtle, narcissus, poppy, rosemary and violet. Flower beds were popular in the courtyards of the rich Romans.

The Middle Ages was a period of decline in gardening. After the fall of Rome, gardening was only to growing medicinal herbs and decorating church altars.

Islamic gardens were built after the model of Persian gardens, with enclosed walls and watercourses dividing the garden into four. Commonly, the center of the garden would have a pool or pavilion. Mosaics and glazed tiles used to decorate elaborate fountains are specific to Islamic gardens. [8]

35. What is a characteristic feature of Roman gardens?

a. Statues and sculptures
b. Flower beds
c. Medicinal herbs
d. Courtyard gardens

36. When did gardening decline?

a. Before the Fall of Rome
b. Gardening did not decline
c. Before the Middle Ages
d. After the Fall of Rome

Questions 37 – 40 refer to the following passage.

Passage 11 - Winged Victory of Samothrace: the Statue of the Gods

Students who read about the "Winged Victory of Samothrace" probably won't be able to picture what this statue looks like. However, almost anyone who knows a little about statues will recognize it when they see it: it is the statue of a winged woman who does not have arms or a head. Even the most famous pieces of art may be recognized by sight but not by name.

This iconic statue is of the Greek goddess Nike, who represented victory and was called Victoria by the Romans. The statue is sometimes called the "Nike of Samothrace." She was often displayed in Greek art as driving a chariot, and her speed or efficiency with the chariot may be what her wings symbolize. It is said that the statue was created around 200 BCE to celebrate a battle that was won at sea. Archaeologists and art historians believe the statue may have originally been part of a temple or other building, even one of the most important temples, Megaloi Theoi, just as many statues were used during that time.

"Winged Victory" does indeed appear to have had arms and a head when it was originally created, and it is unclear why they were removed or lost. Indeed, they have never been discovered, even with all the excavation that has taken place. Many speculate that one of her arms was raised and put to her mouth, as though she was shouting or calling out, which is consistent with the idea of her as a war figure. If the missing pieces were ever to be found, they might give Greek and art historians more of an idea of what Nike represented or how the statue was used.

Learning about pieces of art through details like these can help students remember time frames or locations, as well as learn about the people who occupied them.

37. The author's title says the statue is "of the Gods" because

   a. the statue is very beautiful and even a god would find it beautiful.
   b. the statue is of a Greek goddess, and gods were of primary importance to the Greek.
   c. Nike lead the gods into war.
   d. the statues were used at the temple of the gods and so it belonged to them.

38. The third paragraph states that

   a. the statue is related to war and was probably broken apart by foreign soldiers.
   b. the arms and head of the statue cannot be found because all the excavation has taken place.
   c. speculations have been made about what the entire statue looked like and what it symbolized.
   d. the statue has no arms or head because the sculptor lost them.

39. The author's main purpose in writing this passage is to

   a. demonstrate that art and culture are related and one can teach us about the other
   b. persuade readers to become archaeologists and find the missing pieces of the statue
   c. teach readers about the Greek goddess Nike
   d. to teach readers the name of a statue they probably recognize

40. The author specifies the indirect audience as "students" because

   a. it is probably a student who is taking this test
   b. most young people don't know much about art yet and most young people are students
   c. students read more than people who are not students
   d. the passage is based on a discussion of what we can learn about culture from art

Section IV – Math

1. Simplify 2 1/3 / 1 2/5

   a. 1 2/5
   b. 1 2/3
   c. 1 1/7
   d. 2 2/5

2. 2/3 x 1 4/7 x 5 1/4

   a. 3 1/4
   b. 5 1/2
   c. 6 2/3
   d. 4 2/5

3. Simplify 4 1/5 / 2 1/3

   a. 1 4/5
   b. 2 1/4
   c. 1 3/7
   d. 2 1/4

4. 10/3 x 2 1/4 x 3 1/5

   a. 1 3/4
   b. 24
   c. 7 2/7
   d. 5 1/5

5. Simplify 3 1/9 / 2 2/3

   a. 2 1/5
   b. 2 3/4
   c. 1 1/6
   d. 1 1/4

6. What is -9 + (+6) – (-2)

   a. -3
   b. -1
   c. 5
   d. -5

7. Smith and Simon are playing a card game. Smith will win if a card drawn from a deck of 52 is either a 7 or a diamond, and Simon will win if the drawn card is an even number. Which statement is more likely to be correct?

   a. Simon will win more games.
   b. Smith will win more games.
   c. They have same winning probability.
   d. A decision cannot be made from the provided data.

8. By practicing, a typist increases his typing speed by 2 words per minute daily. If his current typing speed is 18 words per minute and he practice 3 hours a day, then how many hours will he need to practice to attain 40 words per minute?

   a. 27
   b. 30
   c. 33
   d. 36

9. If the speed of a train is 72 kilometers per hour, what distance will it cover in 12 seconds?

   a. 200 m
   b. 220 m
   c. 240 m
   d. 260 m

10. In a class of 83 students, 72 are present. What percent of the students are absent? Provide answer up to two significant digits.

   a. 12
   b. 13
   c. 14
   d. 15

11. A driver traveled from city A to city B in 1 hour and 13 minutes. On the way, he had to stop at 5 traffic signals, with an average time of 80 seconds. If the distance between the cities is 65 kilometers then what was the average driving speed?

   a. 56.42
   b. 58.77
   c. 60.34
   d. 63.25

12. Mr. Micheal runs a factory. His total assets are $256,800 that consists of a building worth $80,500, machinery worth $125.000 and $51,300 cash. After one year what will be the value of his total assets if he has additional cash of $75,600 and the value of his building has increased by 10% per year, and his machinery depreciated by 20% per year?

   a. $24,3450
   b. $25,2450
   c. $26,4150
   d. $27,2350

13. Martin earns $25,000 as basic pay, $500 rent and $860 for medical insurance. He spends 40% of his total earning on food and clothing, 10% on children's education and pays $800 for utility bills. What percent of his earning he is saving?

   a. 54%
   b. 50%
   c. 47%
   d. 44%

14. Prize money of $1,050 is to be shared among top three contestants in ratio of 7:5:3 as 1st, 2nd and 3rd prizes respectively. How much more money will the 1st prize contestant receive than the 3rd prize contestant?

   a. $210
   b. $280
   c. $350
   d. $490

15. The manager of a weaving factory estimates that if 10 machines run on 100% efficiency for 8 hours, they will produce 1450 meters of cloth. Due to some technical problems, 4 machines run of 95% efficiency and the remaining 6 at 90% efficiency. How many meters of cloth can these machines will produce in 8 hours?

   a. 1334 meters
   b. 1310 meters
   c. 1300 meters
   d. 1285 meters

16. A car covers a distance in 3.5 hours at an average speed of 60 km/hr. How much time in hours will a motorbike take to cover this distance at an average speed of 40km/hr?

    a. 4.5
    b. 4.75
    c. 5
    d. 5.25

17. A grandfather is 8 times older than his grandson is now. After 6 years, he will be 5 times older than his grandson will. How old is the grandfather now?

    a. 48
    b. 56
    c. 64
    d. 72

18. Solve for n. 5n + (19 – 2)) = 67.

    a. 21
    b. 10
    c. 15
    d. 7

19. A boy is given 2 apples while his sister is given 8 oranges. What is the ratio between his apples and her oranges?

    a. 1:2
    b. 2:4
    c. 1:4
    d. 2:1

20. A box contains 7 black pencils and 28 blue ones. What is the ratio between the black and blue pens?

    a. 1:4
    b. 2:7
    c. 1:8
    d. 1:9

21. If X + (32 + 356) = 920. What is x?

    a. 450
    b. 388
    c. 532
    d. 623

22. A boy buys 10 candies. The packet contains 3 green candies, 12 red and 9 blue candies. What is the ratio the green, red and blue sweets?

    a. 1:3:4
    b. 1:4:3
    c. 2:3:1
    d. 1:5:4

23. Solve for x. (12 x 12)/x = 12

    a. 12
    b. 13
    c. 8
    d. 14

24. Solve for A. A – (34 x 2) = 18.

    a. 86
    b. 78
    c. 50
    d. 73

25. Solve for X.   X% of 120 = 30.

   a. 15
   b. 12
   c. 4
   d. 25

26. Solve for X. X * 25% of 100 = 76.

   a. 15
   b. 19
   c. 21
   d. 13

27. Solve for X.   X% of 250 = 50.

   a. 30
   b. 35
   c. 25
   d. 20

28. What is the least common multiple of 4 and 3?

   a. 24
   b. 6
   c. 16
   d. 12

29. What is the ratio between 2 gold coins, 6 silver coins and 12 bronze coins?

   a. 2:3:4
   b. 1:2:4
   c. 1:3:4
   d. 2:3:4

30. What is the least common multiple of 8 and 12?

   a. 24
   b. 36
   c. 12
   d. 8

31. Solve for x.   -7 + 3x = 20.

   a. 7
   b. 5
   c. 4
   d. 9

32. What is the least common multiple of 2 and 3?

   a. 2
   b. 4
   c. 6
   d. 3

33. Solve for c, when 124 = 12c - 20.

   a. 6
   b. 12
   c. 10
   d. 15

34. Simplify 3 8/9 + 5 5/6.

   a. 8 13/15
   b. 8 3/9
   c. 9 13/18
   d. 8 12/18

35. Simplify 7 4/5 + 2 2/5.

   a. 5 3/5
   b. 5 1/5
   c. 4 2/5
   d. 5 2/5

36. Translate the following into an equation: three plus a number times 7 equals 42.

   a. 7(3 + X) = 42
   b. 3(X + 7) = 42
   c. 3X + 7 = 42
   d. (3 + 7)X = 42

37. Estimate 5205 / 25

   a. 108
   b. 308
   c. 208
   d. 408

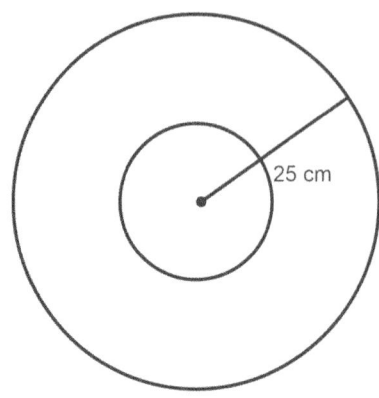

39. What is the distance travelled by the wheel above, when it makes 175 revolutions?

   a. 87.5 π m
   b. 875 π m
   c. 8.75 π m
   d. 8750 π m

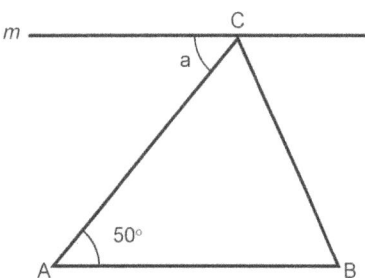

Note: Figure not drawn to scale

38. If the line m is parallel to the side AB of △ABC, what is angle a?

   a. 130°
   b. 25°
   c. 65°
   d. 50°

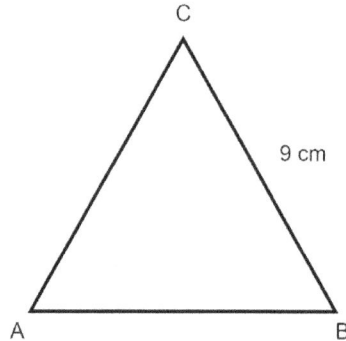

Note: Figure not drawn to scale

40. What is the perimeter of the equilateral △ABC above?

   a. 18 cm
   b. 12 cm
   c. 27 cm
   d. 15 cm

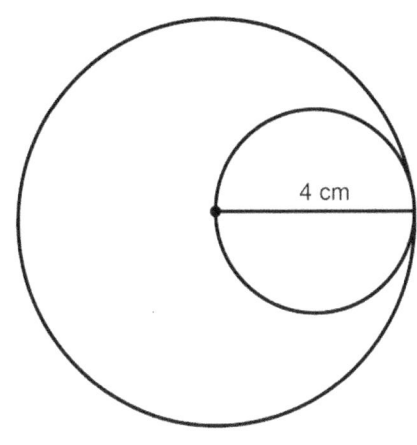

Note: figure not drawn to scale

41. Assuming the diameter of the small circle is the radius of the large circle, what is (area of large circle) - (area of small circle) in the figure above?

    a. 8 π cm²
    b. 10 π cm²
    c. 12 π cm²
    d. 16 π cm²

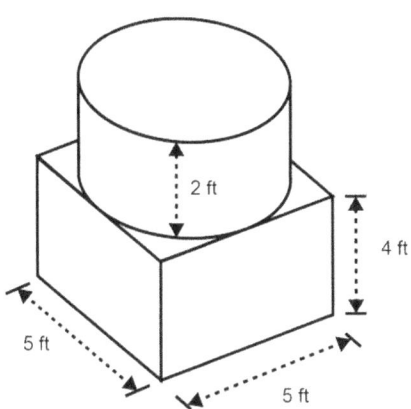

42. What is the approximate total volume of the above solid?

    a. 120 ft³
    b. 100 ft³
    c. 140 ft³
    d. 160 ft³

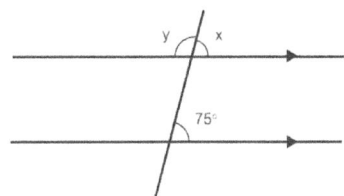

43. What is the value of the angle y?

    a. 25°
    b. 15°
    c. 30°
    d. 105°

44. In a local election at polling station A, 945 voters cast their vote out of 1270 registered voters. At polling station B, 860 cast their vote out of 1050 registered voters and at station C, 1210 cast their vote out of 1440 registered voters. What is the total turnout including all three polling stations?

    a. 70%
    b. 74%
    c. 76%
    d. 80%

45. 3a + 4b x d =? When A = 2, b = 4 and d = 8.

    a. 40
    b. 90
    c. 80
    d. 65

Answer Key

Section I - Verbal Reasoning

1. B
Peculiar and strange are synonyms.

2. B
Tippet and shawl are synonyms.

3. D
Vivid and brilliant are synonyms.

4. B
Semblance and image are synonyms.

5. A
Impregnable and unconquerable are synonyms.

6. A
Jargon and slang are synonyms.

7. A
Render and give are synonyms.

8. B
Intrusive and invasive are synonyms.

9. A
Renowned and popular are synonyms.

10. C
Incoherent and jumbled are synonyms.

11. A
Congenial and pleasant are synonyms.

12. D
Plight and situation are synonyms.

13. A
Berate and criticize are synonyms.

14. C
Construe and interpret are synonyms.

15. D
Scared and terrified are synonyms.

16. A
Demonstrated and presented are synonyms.

17. C
Halt and stop are synonyms.

18. C
Strange and unfamiliar are synonyms.

19. D
Seize and win are synonyms.

20. B
Divulge and tell are synonyms.

21. C
Convection NOUN the vertical movement of heat and moisture.

22. B
Ethanol NOUN a type of alcohol used as fuel.

23. A
Respiratory NOUN relating to respiration; breathing.

24. C
Renewable NOUN capable of being renewed.

25. B
Combustible NOUN capable of burning.

26. D
Conclusive ADJECTIVE providing an end to something; decisive.

27. D
Deftly ADVERB quickly and neatly in action.

28. C
Dupe VERB to swindle, deceive, or trick.

29. D
Designate ADJECTIVE appointed; chosen.

30. A
Dispel VERB to drive away by scattering, or so to cause to vanish; to clear away.

31. B
Frugal ADJECTIVE cheap, economical, thrifty.

22. B
Baubles NOUN a cheap showy ornament.

33. D
Creditors NOUN a person to whom a debt is owed.

34. A
Oratory NOUN the art of public speaking, especially in a formal, expressive, or forceful manner.

35. B
Liquidate VERB to convert assets into cash.

36. A
Hoax NOUN to deceive (someone) by making them believe something which has been maliciously or mischievously fabricated.

37. C
Defective ADJECTIVE imperfect or faulty.

38. B
Grovel VERB to abase oneself before another person.

39. B
Intolerable ADJECTIVE not capable of being borne or endured; not proper or right to be allowed; insufferable; insupportable; unbearable.

40. A
Heirloom NOUN A valued possession that has been passed down through the generations.

Section II – Quantitative Reasoning

1. B
5x + 21 = 66, 5x = 66 – 21 = 45, 5x = 45, x = 45/5 = 9

2. B
Multiples of 3 are 3, 6, 9 and Multiples of 9 are 9, 18, therefore the least common multiple is 9.

3. A
The formula for the volume of a cylinder is = $\prod r^2 h$. Where $\prod$ is 3.142, r is radius of the cross sectional area, and h is the height. So the volume will be = 3.142 × 2.5² × 12 = 235.65 m³.

4. B
215 X 65 = 13,975, or approximately 13,500.

5. D
We understand that each of the n employees earn 's' amount of salary weekly. This means that one employee earns s salary weekly. So; Richard has ns amount of money to employ n employees for a week.

We are asked to find the number of days n employees can be employed with x amount of money. We can do simple direct proportion:

If Richard can employ n employees for

7 days with ns amount of money,

Richard can employ n employees for y days with x amount of money ...
y is the number of days we need to find.

Cross multiply:

y = (x•7)/(ns)

y = 7x/ns

6. B
Average attendance will be 85%

7. B
A driver at a speed of 's' miles per hour can reach his destination in 'h' hours. If his speed increased from 's' to 'x', the driver will reach the destination in h - sh/x hours.

8. B
The number is 41.061. The last digit 1 is less than 5, and so it's discarded. The next digit, 6, is greater than 5 and so is removed and 1 is added to the next digit to the left. Answer = 41.1

9. C
If there are 5 friends and each drink costs $1.89, we can round up to $2 per drink and estimate the total cost at, 5 X $2 = $10.

The actual cost is 5 X $1.89 = $9.45.

10. C
Ratio of people sitting to standing is 24:8, reduce to lowest terms = 3:1

11. A
4,210,987 – 210,078 = 4,000,909, or approximately 4,000,000.

12. A
2^3 = 8 = 1/0.125

$\sqrt{16}$ = 4
3^2 = 9

13. B
10^4 is not equal to 0.1 x 10^5 = 10,000.

14. D
Divide x^5 by x^2 = x^3

15. D
21/28 is the only fraction not equivalent to 3/4.

16. C
3/2 = 1.5
$\sqrt{2}$ = 1.414213
4/3 = 1.333

17. A
1/4 X 100 = 25
25 X 5 = 125

18. C
3X + 3 = 15
X = 4
A – 20 – 4 = 16
B – 4 * $ = 16

19. B
2Y + X will be greater than 2X + Y for any X>0 and Y>0.

20. C
y^2 + 6 = 15
Y = 3

21. D
2ab + 5 = 25
ab = 10
a could be greater or less than 14 (e.g. a = 50 and b = 1/5) or less than 14 (e.g. a = 2 and b = 5).

22. B
0.589/.35 = 1.6828 > 1/2

23. B
.589/.35 = 1.6828 > 2/3.

24. A
4/9 + 3/4 = 43/36 > 24/27

25. B
250 – 20% = 200 – 2% = 196
Total Savings is 250 – 196 = 54.

26. A
X = 135/50 = 2.7 hours < 3.1 hours.

27. B
1 hr. = 60 minutes, at the rate of 1 page per 2 minutes, 60/2 = 30 < 40.

28. B
2X $3 + 1.99 + 1.58 = 9.57 + 3.2% = 9.876 or $9.88
20 − 9.88 = $10.12

29. B
Building: $580,000 + 5.6% = 612,480
Machinery: $255,000 − 15% = 216,750
Cash: $10,000 + 4500 = 14500
Total after 1 year = 643,730

30. A
4% interest is earned in the first year on the initial deposit of $500. In the second year, interest is earned on the initial deposit and the interest earned in the first year.
500 + 4% = 520
520 + 4% = 540.80

$20 was earned in the first year and $20.80 in the second year for a total of $40.80

31. B
(5 + 8 + 2 + 0 + 4)/5 = 3.8

32. B
3/4 = 75% < 80%

33. B
.78 as a fraction = 78/100 < 8/10

34. B
5/6 = 83/100 (approx.) = 83% > 65%

35. A
25% of .8 = .2 < .27

Section III – Reading

1. C
This question tests the reader's summarizing skills. The use of the word "actually" in describing what kind of people poets are, as well as other moments like this, may lead readers to selecting B or D, but the author is giving more information than trying to persuade readers. The author gives no indication that she loves poetry (B) or that people, students specifically (D), should write poems. A is incorrect because the style and content of this paragraph do not match those of a foreword; forewords usually focus on the history or ideas of a specific poem to introduce it more fully and help it stand out against other poems. The author here focuses on several poems and gives broad statements. Instead, she tells a kind of story about poems, giving three very broad time periods in which to discuss them, thereby giving a brief history of poetry, as answer C states.

2. A
This question tests the reader's summarizing skills. Key words in the topic sentences of each of the paragraphs ("oldest," "Renaissance," "modern") should give the reader an idea that the author is moving chronologically. The opening and closing sentence-paragraphs are broad and talk generally. B seems reasonable, but epic poems are mentioned in two paragraphs, eliminating the idea that only new types of poems are used in each paragraph. C is also easily eliminated because the author clearly mentions several different poets, groups of people, and poems. D also seems reasonable, considering that the author does move from older forms of poetry to newer forms, but use of "so (that)" makes this statement false, for the author gives no indication that she is rushing (the paragraphs are about the same size) or that she prefers modern poetry.

3. D
This question tests the reader's attention to detail. The key word is "invented"--it ties together the Mesopotamians, who invented the written word, and the fact that they, as the inventors, also invented and used poetry. The other selections focus on other details mentioned in the passage, such as that the Renaissance's admiration of the Greeks (C) and that Beowulf is in Old English (A). B may seem like an attractive answer because it is unlike the others and because the idea of heroes seems rooted in ancient and early civilizations.

4. B
This question tests the reader's vocabulary and contextualization skills. "Telling" is not an unusual word, but it may be used here in a way that is not familiar to readers, as an adjective rather than a verb in gerund form. A may seem like the obvious answer to a reader looking for a verb to match the use they are familiar with. If the reader understands that the word is being used as an adjective and that A is a ploy, they may opt to select D, "wordy," but it does not make sense in context. C can be easily eliminated, and doesn't have any connection to the paragraph or passage. "Significant" (B) does make sense contextually, especially in relation to the phrase "give insight" used later in the sentence.

5. C
We can infer from the passage that, a virus is too small to be seen with the naked eye. Clearly, if they are too small to be seen with a microscope, then they are too small to be seen with the naked eye.

6. D
Viruses infect all types of organisms. This is taken directly from the passage, "Viruses infect all types of organisms, from animals and plants to bacteria and single-celled organisms."

7. C
The passage does not say exactly how many parts prions and viroids consist of. It does say, "**Unlike** prions and viroids, viruses consist of two or three parts ..." so prions and viroids are NOT like virus. We can therefore infer, they consist of either less than two or more than three parts.

8. B
A common virus spread by coughing and sneezing is Influenza.

9. A
The correct answer because that fact is stated directly in the passage. The passage explains that Anne taught Helen to hear by allowing her to feel the vibrations in her throat.

10. B
We can infer that Anne is a patient teacher because she did not leave or lose her temper when Helen bit or hit her; she just kept trying to teach Helen. Choice B is incorrect because Anne taught Helen to read and talk. Choice C is incorrect because Anne could hear. She was partially blind, not deaf. Choice D is incorrect because it does not have to do with patience.

11. A
The passage states that it was hard for anyone but Anne to understand Helen when she spoke. Choice A is incorrect because the passage does not mention Helen spoke a foreign language. Choice C is incorrect because there is no mention of how quiet or loud Helen's voice was. Choice D is incorrect because we know from reading the passage that Helen did learn to speak.

12. C
The purpose of this text is to explain when meteorologists consider a thunderstorm severe.

The main idea is the first sentence, "The United States National Weather Service classifies thunderstorms as severe when they reach a predetermined level." After the first sentence, the passage explains and elaborates on this idea. Everything is this passage is related to this idea, and there are no other major ideas in this passage that are central to the whole passage.

13. A

From this passage, we can infer that different areas and countries have different criteria for determining a severe storm.

From the passage we can see that most of the US has a criteria of, winds over 50 knots (58 mph or 93 km/h), and hail ¾ inch (2 cm). For the Central US, hail must be 1 inch (2.5 cm) in diameter. In Canada, winds must be 90 km/h or greater, hail 2 centimeters in diameter or greater, and rainfall more than 50 millimeters in 1 hour, or 75 millimeters in 3 hours.

Choice D is incorrect because the Canadian system is the same for hail, 2 centimeters in diameter.

14. C

With hail above the minimum size of 2.5 cm. diameter, the Central Region of the United States National Weather Service would issue a severe thunderstorm warning.

15. A

Low blood sugar occurs both in diabetics and healthy adults.

16. B

None of the statements are the author's opinion.

17. A

The author's purpose is the inform.

18. A

The only statement that is not a detail is, "A doctor can diagnosis this medical condition by asking the patient questions and testing."

19. A

The correct order of ingredients is brown sugar, baking soda and chocolate chips.

20. B

Sturdy: strong, solid in structure or person. In context, Stir in chocolate chips by hand with a *sturdy* wooden spoon.

21. A

Disperse: to scatter in different directions or break up. In context, Stir until the chocolate chips and nuts are evenly *dispersed.*

22. B

You can stop stirring the nuts when they are evenly distributed. From the passage, "Stir until the chocolate chips and nuts are evenly dispersed."

23. D

This question tests the reader's summarization skills. The question is asking very generally about the message of the passage, and the title, "Ways Characters Communicate in Theater," is one indication of that. The other answers A, B, and C are all directly from the text, and therefore readers may be inclined to select one of them, but are too specific to encapsulate the entirety of the passage and its message.

24. B
The paragraph on soliloquies mentions "To be or not to be," and it is from the context of that paragraph that readers may understand that because "To be or not to be" is a soliloquy, Hamlet will be introspective, or thoughtful, while delivering it. It is true that actors deliver soliloquies alone, and may be "solitary" (A), but "thoughtful" (B) is more true to the overall idea of the paragraph. Readers may choose C because drama and theater can be used interchangeably and the passage mentions that soliloquies are unique to theater (and therefore drama), but this answer is not specific enough to the paragraph in question. Readers may pick up on the theme of life and death and Hamlet's true intentions and select that he is "hopeless" (D), but those themes are not discussed either by this paragraph or passage, as a close textual reading and analysis confirms.

25. C
This question tests the reader's grammatical skills. B seems logical, but parenthesis are actually considered to be a stronger break in a sentence than commas are, and along this line of thinking, actually disrupt the sentence more. A and D make comparisons between theater and film that are simply not made in the passage, and may or may not be true. This detail does clarify the statement that asides are most unique to theater by adding that it is not completely unique to theater, which may have been why the author didn't chose not to delete it and instead used parentheses to designate the detail's importance (C).

26. C
This question tests the reader's vocabulary and contextualization skills. A may or may not be true, but focuses on the wrong function of the word "give" and ignores the rest of the sentence, which is more relevant to what the passage is discussing. B and D may also be selected if the reader depends too literally on the word "give," failing to grasp the more abstract function of the word that is the focus of answer C, which also properly acknowledges the entirety of the passage and its meaning.

27. A
Navy SEALS are the maritime component of the United States Special Operations Command (USSOCOM).

28. C
Working underwater separates SEALs from other military units. This is taken directly from the passage.

29. D
SEALs also belong to the Navy and the Coast Guard.

30. A
The CIA also participated. From the passage, the raid was conducted by a "team of 40 *CIA-led* Navy SEALS."

31. A
This sentence is a recommendation.

32. C
Tips for a good night's sleep is the best alternative title for this article.

33. B
Mental activity is helpful for a good night's sleep is cannot be inferred from this article.

34. A
From the passage, one disadvantage of taking naps is they may keep you awake at night.
The earliest forms of gardens emerged from the people's need to grow herbs and vegetables. It was only later that rich individuals created gardens for the purely decorative purpose.

35. A
The ancient Roman gardens are known by their statues and sculptures ... from the first sentence.

36. D
After the fall of Rome, gardening was only for medicinal purposes, AND gardening declined in the Middle Ages, so we can infer gardening declined after the fall of Rome.

37. B
This question tests the reader's summarization skills. A is a very broad statement that may or may not be true, and seems to be in context, but has nothing to do with the passage. The author does mention that the statue was probably used on a temple dedicated to the Greek gods (D), but in no way discusses or argues for the gods' attitude toward or claim on these temples or its faucets. Nike does indeed lead the gods into a war (the Titan war), as C suggests, but this is not mentioned by the passage and students who know this may be drawn to this answer but have not done a close enough analysis of the text that is actually in the passage. B is appropriately expository, and connects the titular emphasis to the idea that the Greek gods are very important to Greek culture.

38. C
This question tests the reader's summarization skills. The test for question C is pulled straight from the paragraph, but is not word for word, so it may seem too obvious to be the right answer. The passage does talk about Nike being the goddess of war, as A states, but the third paragraph only touches on it and it is an inference that soldiers destroyed the statue, when this question is asking specifically for what the third paragraph actually stated. B is also straight from the text, with a minor but key change: the inclusion of the words "all" and "never" are too limiting and the passage does not suggest that these limits exist. If a reader selects D, they are also making an inference that is misguided for this type of question. The paragraph does state that the arms and head are "lost" but does not suggest who lost them.

39. A
This question tests the reader's ability to recognize function in writing. B can be eliminated based on the purpose of the passage, which is expository and not persuasive. The author may or may not feel this way, but the passage does not show evidence of being argumentative for that purpose. C and D are both details found in the text, but neither of them encompasses the entire message of the passage, which has an overall message of learning about culture from art and making guesses about how the two are related, as suggested by A.

40. D
This question tests the reader's ability to understand function within writing. Most of the possible selections are very general statements which may or may not be true. It probably is a student who is taking the test on which this question is featured (A), but the author makes no address to the test taker and is not talking to the audience in terms of the test. Likewise, it may also be true that students read more than adults (C), mandated by schools and grades, but the focus on the verb "read" in the first sentence is too narrow and misses the larger purpose of the passage; the same could be said for selection B. While all the statements could be true, D is the most germane, and infers the purpose of the passage without making assumptions that could be incorrect.

Section IV – Mathematics

1. B
First change all the terms to fractions, therefore, we get 7/3 / 7/5, to divide we need to invert the second fraction, 7/3 x 5/7, and then we cancel out to reduce to the lowest terms, 1/3 x 5/1 = 5/3, convert back to proper fraction to get 1 2/3

2. B
First, convert all the terms to fractions and then cancel out. Therefore, 2/3 x 11/7 x 21/4 = 2/3 x 11/1 x 3/4, 1/3 x 11/1 x 3/2, 1/1 x 11/1 x 1/2 = 11/2 = 5 1/2

3. A
First change all the terms to fractions, therefore, we get 21/5 / 7/3, to divide we need to invert the second fraction, 21/5 x 3/7, and then we cancel out to reduce to the lowest terms, 3/5 x 3/1 = 9/5, convert back to proper fraction to get 1 4/5

4. B
First, convert all the terms to fractions and then cancel out. Therefore, 10/3 x 9/4 x 16/5 = 10/1 x 3/4 x 16/5, 10/1 x 3/1 x 4/5, 2/1 x 3/1 x 4/1 = 24/1 = 24

5. C
First change all the terms to fractions, 28/9 / 8/3, to divide we need to invert the second fraction, 28/9 x 3/8, and then we cancel out to reduce to the lowest terms, 7/3 x 1/2 = 7/6, convert back to proper fraction to get 1 1/6

6. B
+(+) becomes a positive sign and -(-) equals +, therefore -9 + (+6) – (-2) = -9 + 6 + 2 = -3 + 2 = -1

7. B
There are 52 cards. Smith has 16 cards in which he can win. Therefore, his winning probability in a single game will be 16/52. Simon has 20 cards of wining so his probability of winning in single draw is 20/52. Simon will win more games.

8. C
This is an arithmetic series question where the 1st term is 18 and last term is 40. Expressing the question as a series, we have

18, 20, 22, 24, 26, 28, 30, 32, 34, 36, 38, 40
Therefore, after 11 days of practice he attains that 40 word per minute. As he practices 3 hours daily, the total number of hours required will be 33.

9. C
1 hour is equal to 3600 seconds and 1 kilometer is equal to 1000 meters. Therefore, a train covers 72000 meters in 36000 seconds.
Distance covered in 12 seconds = 12 × 72000/3600 = 240 meters.

10. B
Number of absent students = 83 – 72 = 11

Percentage of absent students is found by proportioning the number of absent students to total number of students in the class = 11•100/83 = 13.25

Checking the answers, we round 13.25 to the nearest whole number: 13%

Day	Absent	Present	% Attendance
Monday	5	40	88.88%
Tuesday	9	36	80.00%
Wednesday	4	41	91.11%
Thursday	10	35	77.77%
Friday	6	39	86.66%

11. B
Time taken to travel from A to B in seconds = 3600 + (13 X 60) = 3600 + 780 = 4380 seconds.
Total time spent at traffic signals = 80 X 5 = 400 seconds.
The remaining driving time = 4380 – 400 = 3980 seconds = 3980/3600 = 1.106 hours
The speed will be 65/1.106 = 58.77 km/hr

12. C
Cash assets = 75600
Building assets after one year = 80500 X 1.1 = $88550
Machinery assets after one year = 125000 X 0.8 = 100,000
Total value of assets = 264150

13. C
Total earnings = 25000 + 500 + 860 = $26360
Food and Clothing expenses = 0.4 X 26360 = 10544
Children's education expense = 26360 X 0.1 = $2636
Utility Bills = $800
Savings = 26360 – 10544 – 2636 – 800 = $12380
Percent savings = 100 X 12380/26360 = 47%

14. B
1st prize winner receives, 7 X 1050/15 = $490
3rd price winner receives, 3 X 1050/15 = $210
Difference = 490 – 210 = $280

15. A
At 100% efficiency 1 machine produces 1450/10 = 145 m of cloth.

At 95% efficiency, 4 machines produce 4•145•95/100 = 551 m of cloth.

At 90% efficiency, 6 machines produce 6•145•90/100 = 783 m of cloth.

Total cloth produced by all 10 machines = 551 + 783 = 1334 m

Since the information provided and the question are based on 8 hours, we did not need to use time to reach the answer.

16. D
Distance covered by the car = 60 X 3.5 = 210 km.
Time required by the motorbike = 210/40 = 5.25 hr.

17. C
Let the grandson's age be X and the grandfather's age be Y. According we have,
y = 8x
and
y + 6 = 5(x + 6)
Solving we get y = 64

18. B
5n + (19 – 2)) = 67, 5n + 17 = 67, 5n = 67 -17, 5n = 50, n = 50/5 = 10

19. C
The ratio between apples and oranges is 2 to 8 or 2:8. Bring to the lowest terms by dividing both sides by 2 gives 1:4.

20. A
The ratio between black and blue pens is 7 to 28 or 7:28. Bring to the lowest terms by dividing both sides by 7 gives 1:4.

21. C
32 + 356 = 388. Therefore X + 388 = 920, X = 920 – 388 = 532

22. B
The ratio between green, red and blue candies is 3:12:9. Bring to the lowest terms by dividing the sides by 3 gives 1:4:3.

23. A
12 x 12 = 144, so 144/x =12, X = 12

24. A
34 x 2 = 68, so A – 68 = 18, A = 68 + 18 = 86

25. D
X% of 120 = 30, so X = 30/120 x 100/1 = 300/12 = 25

This questions can be estimated quickly just by looking at the numbers. 30 and 120 are related by, as 4 X 30 = 120. 4 expressed as a percent is 25%. Check quickly, 25% of 120 = 30.

26. B
X * 25% x 100 = 76, therefore, X * 4 = 76, X = 76/4 = 19

27. D
X% of 250 = 50, so X = 50/250 x 100/1= 100/5 = 20

28. D
Multiples of 3 are 3, 6, 9, 12 and Multiples of 4 are 4, 8, 12, Therefore the least common multiple is 12.

This can be estimated quickly. 3 is a prime number so the only possible multiples of 3 and any other number, say X, will be 3X.

29. C
The ratio between gold, silver and bronze coins is 2:6:12. Bring to the lowest terms by dividing each side by 2 gives 1:3:4.

30. A
Multiples of 8 are 8, 16, 24 and multiples of 12 are 12, 24, 36, so the least common multiple is 24.

31. D
3x = 20 + 7 = 27, x = 27/3, x = 9.

32. C
Multiples of 2 are 2, 4, 6 and Multiples of 3 are 3, 6, so the least common is 6.

33. B
124 = 12c - 20, 124 + 20 = 12c, 144 = 12c, c = 144/12 = 12.

34. C
Add the whole numbers and then add the fractions, therefore 3 + 5 {8/9 + 5/6}, then find a common denominator for the fractions 8 {16/18 + 15/18} = 8 31/18, then simplify to 9 13/18

35. D
Subtract the whole numbers and then subtract the fractions, therefore 7 - 2 {4/5 - 2/5}, the fractions has a common denominator, so
5 (4-2/5) = 5 2/5.

36. A
Three plus a number times 7 equals 42. Let X be the number.
(3 + X) times 7 = 42
7(3 + X) = 42

37. C
5205 / 25 = 208.20 or, about 208.

38. D
Two parallel lines(m & side AB) intersected by side AC
a = 50° (interior angles)

39. A
The wheel travels 2πr distance when it makes one revolution. Here, r stands for the radius. The radius is given as 25 cm in the figure. So,

2πr = 2π•25 = 50π cm is the distance travelled in one revolution.

In 175 revolutions: 175•50π = 8750π cm is travelled.

We are asked to find the distance in meter.

1 m = 100 cm So;

8750π cm = 8750π / 100 = 87.5π m

40. C
Equilateral triangle with 9 cm sides
Perimeter = 9+9+9
= 27 cm.

41. C
In the figure, we are given a large circle and a small circle inside it; with the diameter equal to the radius of the large one. The diameter of the small circle is 4 cm. This means that its radius is 2 cm. Since the diameter of the small circle is the radius of the large circle, the radius of the large circle is 4 cm. The area of a circle is calculated by: πr² where r is the radius.

Area of the small circle: π(2)² = 4π

Area of the large circle: π(4)² = 16π

The difference area is found by:

Area of the large circle - Area of the small circle = 16π - 4π = 12π

42. C
Volume of a cylinder is π x r² x h
Diameter = 5 ft. so radius is 2.5 ft.
Volume of the cylinder = π x 2.5² x 2
= π x 6.25 x 2 = 12.5 π
Approximate π to 3.142
Volume of the cylinder = 39.25

Volume of a rectangle = height X width X length.
= 5 X 5 X 4 = 100

Total volume = Volume of rectangular solid + volume of cylinder
Total volume = 100 + 39.25
Total volume = 139.25 ft³ or approximately 140 ft³

43. D
Two parallel lines intersected by a third line with angles of 75°
x = 75° (corresponding angles)
x + y = 180°(supplementary angles)
y = 180° - 75°
y = 105°

44. D
To find the total turnout in all three polling stations, we need to proportion the number of voters to the number of all registered voters.

Total number of voters = 945 + 860 + 1210 = 3015

Total number of registered voters = 1270 + 1050 + 1440 = 3760

Percentage turnout in all three polling stations = 3015•100/3760 = 80.19%

Check the answer, ound 80.19 to the nearest whole number: 80%

45. C
Substitute the known terms, (3 x 2) + (4 x 4) x 8 =, 6 + 4 x 8=, 10 x 8 = 80

Practice Test Questions Set 2

The questions below are not the same as you will find on the ISEE® - that would be too easy! And nobody knows what the questions will be and they change all the time. Below are general questions that cover the same subject areas as the ISEE®. So, while the format and exact wording of the questions may differ slightly, and change from year to year, if you can answer the questions below, you will have no problem with the ISEE®.

For the best results, take these Practice Test Questions as if it were the real exam. Set aside time when you will not be disturbed, and a location that is quiet and free of distractions. Read the instructions carefully, read each question carefully, and answer to the best of your ability.
Use the bubble answer sheets provided. When you have completed the Practice Questions, check your answer against the Answer Key and read the explanation provided.

Do not attempt more than one set of practice test questions in one day. After completing the first practice test, wait two or three days before attempting the second set of questions.

Section I – Verbal Reasoning

Questions: 40 **Time:** 20 Minutes

Section II – Quantitative Reasoning

Questions: 35 **Time:** 35 Minutes

Section III – Reading

Questions: 40 **Time:** 40 Minutes

Section IV – Mathematics

Questions: 45 **Time:** 40 Minutes

Verbal Reasoning

	A	B	C	D	E		A	B	C	D	E
1	○	○	○	○	○	21	○	○	○	○	○
2	○	○	○	○	○	22	○	○	○	○	○
3	○	○	○	○	○	23	○	○	○	○	○
4	○	○	○	○	○	24	○	○	○	○	○
5	○	○	○	○	○	25	○	○	○	○	○
6	○	○	○	○	○	26	○	○	○	○	○
7	○	○	○	○	○	27	○	○	○	○	○
8	○	○	○	○	○	28	○	○	○	○	○
9	○	○	○	○	○	29	○	○	○	○	○
10	○	○	○	○	○	30	○	○	○	○	○
11	○	○	○	○	○	31	○	○	○	○	○
12	○	○	○	○	○	32	○	○	○	○	○
13	○	○	○	○	○	33	○	○	○	○	○
14	○	○	○	○	○	34	○	○	○	○	○
15	○	○	○	○	○	35	○	○	○	○	○
16	○	○	○	○	○	36	○	○	○	○	○
17	○	○	○	○	○	37	○	○	○	○	○
18	○	○	○	○	○	38	○	○	○	○	○
19	○	○	○	○	○	39	○	○	○	○	○
20	○	○	○	○	○	40	○	○	○	○	○

Quantitative Reasoning

	A	B	C	D	E		A	B	C	D	E
1						21					
2						22					
3						23					
4						24					
5						25					
6						26					
7						27					
8						28					
9						29					
10						30					
11						31					
12						32					
13						33					
14						34					
15						35					
16											
17											
18											
19											
20											

Reading Comprehension

	A B C D E		A B C D E
1	○ ○ ○ ○ ○	21	○ ○ ○ ○ ○
2	○ ○ ○ ○ ○	22	○ ○ ○ ○ ○
3	○ ○ ○ ○ ○	23	○ ○ ○ ○ ○
4	○ ○ ○ ○ ○	24	○ ○ ○ ○ ○
5	○ ○ ○ ○ ○	25	○ ○ ○ ○ ○
6	○ ○ ○ ○ ○	26	○ ○ ○ ○ ○
7	○ ○ ○ ○ ○	27	○ ○ ○ ○ ○
8	○ ○ ○ ○ ○	28	○ ○ ○ ○ ○
9	○ ○ ○ ○ ○	29	○ ○ ○ ○ ○
10	○ ○ ○ ○ ○	30	○ ○ ○ ○ ○
11	○ ○ ○ ○ ○	31	○ ○ ○ ○ ○
12	○ ○ ○ ○ ○	32	○ ○ ○ ○ ○
13	○ ○ ○ ○ ○	33	○ ○ ○ ○ ○
14	○ ○ ○ ○ ○	34	○ ○ ○ ○ ○
15	○ ○ ○ ○ ○	35	○ ○ ○ ○ ○
16	○ ○ ○ ○ ○	36	○ ○ ○ ○ ○
17	○ ○ ○ ○ ○	37	○ ○ ○ ○ ○
18	○ ○ ○ ○ ○	38	○ ○ ○ ○ ○
19	○ ○ ○ ○ ○	39	○ ○ ○ ○ ○
20	○ ○ ○ ○ ○	40	○ ○ ○ ○ ○

Mathematics

1. A B C D
2. A B C D
3. A B C D
4. A B C D
5. A B C D
6. A B C D
7. A B C D
8. A B C D
9. A B C D
10. A B C D
11. A B C D
12. A B C D
13. A B C D
14. A B C D
15. A B C D
16. A B C D
17. A B C D
18. A B C D
19. A B C D
20. A B C D
21. A B C D
22. A B C D
23. A B C D
24. A B C D
25. A B C D
26. A B C D
27. A B C D
28. A B C D
29. A B C D
30. A B C D
31. A B C D
32. A B C D
33. A B C D
34. A B C D
35. A B C D
36. A B C D
37. A B C D
38. A B C D
39. A B C D
40. A B C D
41. A B C D
42. A B C D
43. A B C D
44. A B C D
45. A B C D

Section I – Verbal Reasoning

1. COMPETENT

   a. Pensive
   b. Able
   c. Allow
   d. Honest

2. ANTIDOTE

   a. Cure
   b. Lure
   c. Craft
   d. Affiliation

3. CONSENSUS

   a. Quality
   b. Compensation
   c. Agreement
   d. Command

4. MAGNIFY

   a. Amplify
   b. Trace
   c. Shade
   d. Agility

5. IMMACULATE

   a. Haphazard
   b. Perfect
   c. Clean
   d. Payment

6. VIABLE

   a. Haste
   b. Complete
   c. Feasible
   d. Exceptional

7. RATIONALE

   a. Deduct
   b. Reason
   c. Congenial
   d. Errant

8. TINGE

   a. Touch
   b. Spot
   c. Slur
   d. Rant

9. GIST

   a. Context
   b. Flourish
   c. Summary
   d. Speculation

10. INSTIGATE

   a. Correct
   b. Solute
   c. Initiate
   d. Lament

11. EXPERTISE

   a. Specialty
   b. Institutionalize
   c. Accentuate
   d. Brazen

12. FERTILE
   a. Fruitful
   b. Vacant
   c. Overstuffed
   d. Poor

13. ROWDY
   a. Noisy
   b. Rich
   c. Ancient
   d. Crazy

14. COURTEOUS
   a. Polite
   b. Exceptional
   c. Loving
   d. Loyal

15. LEAN
   a. Thin
   b. Straight
   c. Lazy
   d. Blank

16. AUDACIOUS
   a. Bored
   b. Daring
   c. Flighty
   d. Outrageous

17. CONSTITUTE
   a. Establish
   b. Inaugurate
   c. Accomplish
   d. Embellish

18. CORRUPT
   a. Unscrupulous
   b. Ethical
   c. Unimaginable
   d. Impregnable

19. DISPENSE
   a. Distribute
   b. Annoy
   c. Collect
   d. Advise

20. DURATION
   a. Speed
   b. Length
   c. Width
   d. Height

Fill in the blank.

21. Her _____ talent wowed the audience during the contest.
   a. Ugly
   b. Extraordinary
   c. Plain
   d. Ordinary

22. Jean was _____ when her little brother destroyed her favorite doll.
   a. Happy
   b. Lonely
   c. Angry
   d. Surprised

23. We will _____ about our scores on the pop quiz.

   a. Ask
   b. Complain
   c. Suggest
   d. Command

24. The car accident was an/a _____ experience the victims want to forget.

   a. Terrible
   b. Pleasant
   c. Wonderful
   d. Unforgettable

25. Cinderella's _____ stepmother failed in the end.

   a. Understanding
   b. Happy
   c. Evil
   d. Supportive

26. Her business success showed that she was very _____.

   a. Slow
   b. Astute
   c. Ignorant
   d. Heinous

27. It is boring and I would rather not go, but the ceremony is _____.

   a. Mandatory
   b. Optional
   c. Adaptable
   d. None of the above.

28. We don't want to hear the whole thing. Just the _____ facts please.

   a. Irrelevant
   b. Erroneous
   c. Relevant
   d. Trivial

29. She works in a cubicle answering the phone all day. Her doctor says she is too _____.

   a. Sedentary
   b. Active
   c. Morbid
   d. None of the Above.

30. I don't know why he is being so nice. I am sure he has a/an _____ motive.

   a. Inferior
   b. Ulterior
   c. Simplistic
   d. Unfortunate

31. We cannot reveal the source. It was posted by _____.

   a. Anonymous
   b. Author
   c. Someone
   d. Nobody

32. I have never seen anyone so rude. His behavior was _____.

   a. Monstrous
   b. Perfect
   c. Atrocious
   d. Suspicious

33. I see that sign everywhere. It is much more _____ than I thought.

   a. Prelude
   b. Prevalent
   c. Ratify
   d. Rational

34. Her attitude was very _____.

   a. Idle
   b. Nonchalant
   c. Portly
   d. Portend

35. The water in the pond has been sitting for so long it is _____.

   a. Stagnant
   b. Sediment
   c. Stupor
   d. Residue

36. I cannot wait to try some of the _____ dishes served in the new restaurant.

   a. Succor
   b. Expensive
   c. Variable
   d. Delicious

37. Can you _____ the character of Juliet in the play?

   a. Report
   b. Describe
   c. State
   d. Draw

38. The soldiers _____ the rebel's camp.

   a. Ruined
   b. Ended
   c. Fixed
   d. Conquered

39. There is a big _____ in Esther and Pete's grades.

   a. Complication
   b. Dissimilarity
   c. Minus
   d. Increase

40. I can _____ my goals in life when I study hard.

   a. Finish
   b. Forget
   c. Effect
   d. Achieve

Section II – Quantitative Reasoning

1. Simplify 6 3/5 – 4 4/5

   a. 2 4/5
   b. 2 3/5
   c. 2 9/5
   d. 1 1/5

2. Estimate 46,227 + 101,032.

   a. 14,700
   b. 147,000
   c. 14,700,000
   d. 104,700

3. Solve √121

a. 11
b. 12
c. 21
d. None of the above

4. Kate's father is 32 years older than Kate is. In 5 years, he will be five times older. How old is Kate?

a. 2
b. 3
c. 5
d. 6

5. If Lynn can type a page in p minutes, what portion of the page can she do in 5 minutes?

a. 5/p
b. p - 5
c. p + 5
d. p/5

6. If Sally can paint a house in 4 hours, and John can paint the same house in 6 hours, how long will it take for both of them to paint the house together?

a. 2 hours and 24 minutes
b. 3 hours and 12 minutes
c. 3 hours and 44 minutes
d. 4 hours and 10 minutes

7. Sales of a local football team's season tickets have gone up 10% in the current season to 880 tickets. Last year, they sold X season tickets. X equals:

a. 700
b. 800
c. 880
d. 928

8. In an office, 12 employees can finish a task in 7 hours. If two of them are absent, how much more time will they have to work to complete the task?

a. 10 minutes
b. 12 minutes
c. 15 minutes
d. 20 minutes

9. A bullet train traveling at 300km/hr passes station A at 8:56 pm. What time will the train reach station B, which is 45km away?

a. 9:03 pm
b. 9:05 pm
c. 9:07 pm
d. 9:10 pm

10. There were some oranges in a basket, by adding 8/5 of these the total became 130. How many oranges were in the basket before?

a. 60
b. 50
c. 40
d. 35

11. In a 30-minute test, there are 40 problems. A student solved 28 problems in first 25 minutes. How many seconds should she give to each of the remaining problems?

   a. 20 seconds
   b. 23 seconds
   c. 25 seconds
   d. 27 seconds

12. 2/3 of what number added to 10 is 3 times 15?

   a. 50
   b. 52.5
   c. 65
   d. 72.8

13. What number is 25 more than 1/3 of 27?

   a. 34
   b. -16
   c. 20
   d. 18

14. Richard sold 12 shirts for total revenue of $336 at 8% profit. What is the purchase price of each shirt?

   a. $25.75
   b. $24.50
   c. $23.75
   d. $22.50

15. If we know it takes 12 men to operate four machines, how many are required to operate 20 machines?

   a. 6
   b. 20
   c. 60
   d. 9

16. What number is 10 less than 5 squared?

   a. 25
   b. 10
   c. 15
   d. 40

17. What number divided by 5 is 2/3 of 100?

   a. 333.33
   b. 444.44
   c. 250
   d. 100

18.

Column A	Column B
.97 - .49	.76 + .21

   a. Column A is greater
   b. Column B is greater
   c. The quantities are equal
   d. The relationship cannot be determined

19.

Column A	Column B
1/3 + 1/5 + 3/6	2/3 + 3/4

   a. Column A is greater
   b. Column B is greater
   c. The quantities are equal
   d. The relationship cannot be determined

20.

Column A	Column B
2/8 + 5/6	6/8 + 4/2

    a. Column A is greater
    b. Column B is greater
    c. The quantities are equal
    d. The relationship cannot be determined

21.

Column A	Column B
Martin's taxes	$290

Martin earns $1800 per month and pays 16% taxes.

    a. Column A is greater
    b. Column B is greater
    c. The quantities are equal
    d. The relationship cannot be determined

22.

Column A	Column B
The area of a square with 5 cm. sides	The area of a rectangle with sides 2 cm and 10 cm.

    a. Column A is greater
    b. Column B is greater
    c. The quantities are equal
    d. The relationship cannot be determined

23.

Column A	Column B
The area of a circle with 19 cm. radius	The area of a square with 25 cm sides

    a. Column A is greater
    b. Column B is greater
    c. The quantities are equal
    d. The relationship cannot be determined

24.

Column A	Column B
The area of a circle with 9 cm. radius	The area of a triangle with 5 cm base and 10 cm height

    a. Column A is greater
    b. Column B is greater
    c. The quantities are equal
    d. The relationship cannot be determined

25.

Column A	Column B
40% of 500	12% of 1350

    a. Column A is greater
    b. Column B is greater
    c. The quantities are equal
    d. The relationship cannot be determined

26.

Column A	Column B
18% of 150	22% of 60

  a. Column A is greater
  b. Column B is greater
  c. The quantities are equal
  d. The relationship cannot be determined

27.

Column A	Column B
15% of 50	12% of 75

  a. Column A is greater
  b. Column B is greater
  c. The quantities are equal
  d. The relationship cannot be determined

28.

Column A	Column B
.234 + .673	.990 - .378

  a. Column A is greater
  b. Column B is greater
  c. The quantities are equal
  d. The relationship cannot be determined

29.

Column A	Column B
Probability of drawing a red ball.	Probability of drawing a yellow ball.

There are 6 red balls and 4 yellow balls in a box.

  a. Column A is greater
  b. Column B is greater
  c. The quantities are equal
  d. The relationship cannot be determined

30.

Column A	Column B
Probability of drawing a red ball.	Probability of drawing a green ball.

There are 6 red balls, 5 green balls and 4 yellow balls in a box.

  a. Column A is greater
  b. Column B is greater
  c. The quantities are equal
  d. The relationship cannot be determined

31.

Column A	Column B
Cost of John's sweater.	Cost of Jill's Jacket

Jack bought a $75 sweater at 22% off and Jill bought a $100 jacket at 35% off.

   a. Column A is greater
   b. Column B is greater
   c. The quantities are equal
   d. The relationship cannot be determined

32.

Column A	Column B
2/5	.993 - .34

   a. Column A is greater
   b. Column B is greater
   c. The quantities are equal
   d. The relationship cannot be determined

33.

Column A	Column B
1/3 + 4/7	6.93 - 6.34

   a. Column A is greater
   b. Column B is greater
   c. The quantities are equal
   d. The relationship cannot be determined

34.

Column A	Column B
.25 + .67	.89 - .34

   a. Column A is greater
   b. Column B is greater
   c. The quantities are equal
   d. The relationship cannot be determined

35.

Column A	Column B
.13 + .64	.62 - .14

   a. Column A is greater
   b. Column B is greater
   c. The quantities are equal
   d. The relationship cannot be determined

Section III - Reading

Questions 1-4 refer to the following passage.

Passage 1 - The Respiratory System

The respiratory system's function is to allow oxygen exchange through all parts of the body. The anatomy or structure of the exchange system, and the uses of the exchanged gases, varies depending on the organism. In humans and other mammals, for example, the anatomical features of the respiratory system include airways, lungs, and the respiratory muscles. Molecules of oxygen and carbon dioxide are passively exchanged, by diffusion, between the gaseous external environment and the blood. This exchange process occurs in the alveolar region of the lungs.

Other animals, such as insects, have respiratory systems with very simple anatomical features, and in amphibians even the skin plays a vital role in gas exchange. Plants also have respiratory systems but the direction of gas exchange can be opposite to that of animals.

The respiratory system can also be divided into physiological, or functional, zones. These include the conducting zone (the region for gas transport from the outside atmosphere to just above the alveoli), the transitional zone, and the respiratory zone (the alveolar region where gas exchange occurs).

http://en.wikipedia.org/wiki/Respiratory_system.

1. What can we infer from the first paragraph in this passage?

    a. Human and mammal respiratory systems are the same.
    b. The lungs are an important part of the respiratory system.
    c. The respiratory system varies in different mammals.
    d. Oxygen and carbon dioxide are passive exchanged by the respiratory system.

2. What is the process by which molecules of oxygen and carbon dioxide are passively exchanged?

    a. Transfusion
    b. Affusion
    c. Diffusion
    d. Respiratory confusion

3. What organ plays an important role in gas exchange in amphibians?

   a. The skin
   b. The lungs
   c. The gills
   d. The mouth

4. What are the three physiological zones of the respiratory system?

   a. Conducting, transitional, respiratory zones
   b. Redacting, transitional, circulatory zones
   c. Conducting, circulatory, inhibiting zones
   d. Transitional, inhibiting, conducting zones

Questions 5-8 refer to the following passage.

ABC Electric Warranty

ABC Electric Company warrants that its products are free from defects in material and workmanship. Subject to the conditions and limitations set forth below, ABC Electric will, at its option, either repair or replace any part of its products that prove defective due to improper workmanship or materials.

This limited warranty does not cover any damage to the product from improper installation, accident, abuse, misuse, natural disaster, insufficient or excessive electrical supply, abnormal mechanical or environmental conditions, or any unauthorized disassembly, repair, or modification.

This limited warranty also does not apply to any product on which the original identification information has been altered, or removed, has not been handled or packaged correctly, or has been sold as second-hand.

This limited warranty covers only repair, replacement, refund or credit for defective ABC Electric products, as provided above.

5. I tried to repair my ABC Electric blender, but could not, so can I get it repaired under this warranty?

   a. Yes, the warranty still covers the blender.
   b. No, the warranty does not cover the blender.
   c. Uncertain. ABC Electric may or may not cover repairs under this warranty.

6. My ABC Electric fan is not working. Will ABC Electric provide a new one or repair this one?

   a. ABC Electric will repair my fan
   b. ABC Electric will replace my fan
   c. ABC Electric could either replace or repair my fan or I can request either a replacement or a repair.

7. My stove was damaged in a flood. Does this warranty cover my stove?

   a. Yes, it is covered.
   b. No, it is not covered.
   c. It may or may not be covered.
   d. ABC Electric will decide if it is covered.

8. Which of the following is an example of improper workmanship?

   a. Missing parts
   b. Defective parts
   c. Scratches on the front
   d. None of the above

Questions 9 – 11 refer to the following passage.

Passage 2 – Mythology

The main characters in myths are usually gods or supernatural heroes. As sacred stories, rulers and priests have traditionally endorsed their myths and as a result, myths have a close link with religion and politics. In the society where a myth originates, the natives believe the myth is a true account of the remote past. In fact, many societies have two categories of traditional narrative—(1) "true stories," or myths, and (2) "false stories," or fables.

Myths generally take place during a primordial age, when the world was still young, before achieving its current form. These stories explain how the world gained its current form and why the culture developed its customs, institutions, and taboos. Closely related to myth are legend and folktale. Myths, legends, and folktales are different types of traditional stories. Unlike myths, folktales can take place at any time and any place, and the natives do not usually consider them true or sacred. Legends, on the other hand, are similar to myths in that many people have traditionally considered them true. Legends take place in a more recent time, when the world was much as it is today. In addition, legends generally feature humans as their main characters, whereas myths have superhuman characters.

https://en.wikipedia.org/wiki/Mythology.

9. We can infer from this passage that

a. Folktales took place in a time far past, before civilization covered the earth.

b. Humankind uses myth to explain how the world was created.

c. Myths revolve around gods or supernatural beings; the local community usually accepts these stories as not true.

d. The only difference between a myth and a legend is the time setting of the story.

10. The main purpose of this passage is

a. To distinguish between many types of traditional stories, and explain the back-ground of some traditional story categories.

b. To determine whether myths and legends might be true accounts of history.

c. To show the importance of folktales how these traditional stories made life more bearable in harder times.

d. None of the Above.

11. How are folktales different from myths?

a. Folktales and myth are the same.

b. Folktales are not true and generally not sacred and take place anytime.

c. Myths are not true and generally not sacred and take place anytime.

d. Folktales explained the formation of the world and myths do not.

Getting Started

A Better Score Is Possible 6
Types of Multiple Choice 9
Multiple Choice Step-by-Step 12
Tips for Reading the Instructions 13
General Multiple Choice Tips 14
Multiple Choice Strategy Practice 20
Answer Key 39

12. Based on the partial Table of Contents above, what is this book about?

a. How to answer multiple choice questions

b. Different types of multiple choice questions

c. How to write a test

d. None of the above

Questions 13-16 refer to the following passage.

Passage 3 – Myths, Legend and Folklore

Cultural historians draw a distinction between myth, legend and folktale simply as a way to group traditional stories. However, in many cultures, drawing a sharp line between myths and legends is not that simple. Instead of dividing their traditional stories into myths, legends, and folktales, some cultures divide them into two categories. The first category roughly corresponds to folktales, and the second is one that combines myths and legends. Similarly, we can not always separate myths from folktales. One society might consider a story true, making it a myth. Another society may believe the story is fiction, which makes it a folktale. In fact, when a myth loses its status as part of a religious system, it often takes on traits more typical of folktales, with its formerly divine characters now appearing as human heroes, giants, or fairies. Myth, legend, and folktale are only a few of the categories of traditional stories. Other categories include anecdotes and some kinds of jokes. Traditional stories, in turn, are only one category within the larger category of folklore, which also includes items such as gestures, costumes, and music.

13. The main idea of this passage is that

a. Myths, fables, and folktales are not the same thing, and each describes a specific type of story.

b. Traditional stories can be categorized in different ways by different people.

c. Cultures use myths for religious purposes, and when this is no longer true, the people forget and discard these myths.

d. Myths can never become folk tales, because one is true, and the other is false.

14. The terms myth and legend are

a. Categories that are synonymous with true and false.

b. Categories that group traditional stories according to certain characteristics.

c. Interchangeable, because both terms mean a story that is passed down from generation to generation.

d. Meant to distinguish between a story that involves a hero and a cultural message and a story meant only to entertain.

15. Traditional story categories not only include myths and legends, but

a. Can also include gestures, since some cultures passed these down before the written and spoken word.

b. In addition, folklore refers to stories involving fables and fairy tales.

c. These story categories can also include folk music and traditional dress.

d. Traditional stories themselves are a part of the larger category of folklore, which may also include costumes, gestures, and music.

16. This passage shows that

a. There is a distinct difference between a myth and a legend, although both are folktales.

b. Myths are folktales, but folktales are not myths.

c. Myths, legends, and folktales play an important part in tradition and the past, and are a rich and colorful part of history.

d. Most cultures consider myths to be true.

Questions 17 - 21 refer to the following passage.

Passage 4 – Trees I

Trees are an important part of the natural landscape because they prevent erosion and protect ecosystems in and under their branches. Trees also play an important role in producing oxygen and reducing carbon dioxide in the atmosphere, as well as moderating ground temperatures. Trees are important elements in landscaping and agriculture, both for their visual appeal and for their crops, such as apples, and other fruit. Wood from trees is a building material, and a primary energy source in many developing countries. Trees also play a role in many of the world's mythologies.

https://en.wikipedia.org/wiki/tree.

17. What are two reasons trees are important in the natural landscape?

a. They prevent erosion and produce oxygen.

b. They produce fruit and are important elements in landscaping.

c. Trees are not important in the natural landscape.

d. Trees produce carbon dioxide and prevent erosion.

18. What kind of ecosystems do trees protect?

a. Trees do not protect ecosystems.

b. Weather sheltered ecosystems.

c. Ecosystems around the base and under the branches.

d. All of the above.

19. Which of the following is true?

   a. Trees provide a primary food source in the developing world.
   b. Trees provide a primary building material in the developing world.
   c. Trees provide a primary energy source in the developing world.
   d. Trees provide a primary oxygen source in the developing world.

20. Why are trees important for agriculture?

   a. Because of their crops.
   b. Because they shelter ecosystems.
   c. Because they are a source of energy.
   d. Because of their visual appeal.

21. What do trees do to the atmosphere?

   a. Trees produce carbon dioxide and reduce oxygen.
   b. Trees product oxygen and carbon dioxide.
   c. Trees reduce oxygen and carbon dioxide.
   d. Trees produce oxygen and reduce carbon dioxide.

Questions 22 - 25 refer to the following passage.

Passage 5 Women and Advertising

Only in the last few generations have media messages been so widespread and so readily seen, heard, and read by so many people. Advertising is an important part of both selling and buying anything from soap to cereal to jeans. For whatever reason, more consumers are women than are men. Media message are subtle but powerful, and more attention has been paid lately to how these message affect women.

Of all the products that women buy, makeup, clothes, and other stylistic or cosmetic products are among the most popular. This means that companies focus their advertising on women, promising them that their product will make her feel, look, or smell better than the next company's product will. This competition has resulted in advertising that is more and more ideal and less and less possible for everyday women. However, because women do look to these ideals and the products they represent as how they can potentially become, many women have developed unhealthy attitudes about themselves when they have failed to become those ideals.

In recent years, more companies have tried to change advertisements to be healthier for women. This includes featuring models of more sizes and addressing a huge outcry against unfair tools such as airbrushing and photo editing. There is debate about what the right balance between real and ideal is, because fashion is also considered art and some changes are made to purposefully elevate fashionable products and signify that they are creative, innovative, and the work of individual people. Artists want their freedom protected as much as women do, and advertising agencies are often caught in the middle.

Some claim that the companies who make these changes are not doing enough. Many people worry that there are still not enough models of different sizes and different ethnicities. Some people claim that companies use this healthier type of advertisement not for the good of women, but because they would like to sell products to the women who are looking for these kinds of messages. This is also a hard balance to find: companies do need to make money, and women do need to feel respected.

While the focus of this change has been on women, advertising can also affect men, and this change will hopefully be a lesson on media for all consumers.

22. The second paragraph states that advertising focuses on women

    a. in order to shape what the ideal should be.
    b. because women buy makeup.
    c. because women are easily persuaded.
    d. because of the types of products that women buy.

23. According to the passage, fashion artists and female consumers are at odds because

    a. there is a debate going on and disagreement drives people apart.
    b. both of them are trying to protect their freedom to do something.
    c. artists want to elevate their products above the reach of women.
    d. women are creative, innovative, individual people.

24. The author uses the phrase "for whatever reason" in this passage in order to

    a. keep the focus of the paragraph on media messages and not on the differences between men and women
    b. show that the reason for this is unimportant
    c. argue that it is stupid that more women are consumers than men
    d. show that he or she is tired of talking about why media messages are important

25. This passage suggests that

    a. advertising companies are still working on making their messages better

    b. all advertising companies seek to be more approachable for women

    c. women are only buying from companies that respect them

    d. artists could stop producing fashionable products if they feel bullied

Questions 26 - 28 refer to the following passage.

Lowest Price Guarantee

Get it for less. Guaranteed!

ABC Electric will beat any advertised price by 10% of the difference.

    1) If you find a lower advertised price, we will beat it by 10% of the difference.

    2) If you find a lower advertised price within 30 days* of your purchase we will beat it by 10% of the difference.

    3) If our own price is reduced within 30 days* of your purchase, bring in your receipt and we will refund the difference.

*14 days for computers, monitors, printers, laptops, tablets, cellular & wireless devices, home security products, projectors, camcorders, digital cameras, radar detectors, portable DVD players, DJ and pro-audio equipment, and air conditioners.

26. I bought a radar detector 15 days ago and saw an ad for the same model only cheaper. Can I get 10% of the difference refunded?

    a. Yes. Since it is less than 30 days, you can get 10% of the difference refunded.

    b. No. Since it is more than 14 days, you cannot get 10% of the difference re-funded.

    c. It depends on the cashier.

    d. Yes. You can get the difference refunded.

27. I bought a flat-screen TV for $500 10 days ago and found an advertisement for the same TV, at another store, on sale for $400. How much will ABC refund under this guarantee?

    a. $100

    b. $110

    c. $10

    d. $400

28. What is the purpose of this passage?

   a. To inform
   b. To educate
   c. To persuade
   d. To entertain

Questions 29 - 32 refer to the following passage.

Passage 6 - Pearl Harbor

A Day That Will Live in Infamy! Attack on Pearl Harbor
In 1941, the world was at war. The United States was trying to stay out of the conflict. In Europe, the countries of Germany and Italy had formed an alliance to expand their land and territory. Germany had already taken over Poland, Denmark, and parts of France. They were heading next toward England and due to all the fighting in Europe, there were battles taking place as far south as North Africa, where the German and Italian armies were fighting the British.

This got even worse when the Asian nation of Japan formed an alliance with Germany and Italy. Together, the three countries called themselves, the AXIS. Now, the war was in the Pacific as well as in Europe and Northern Africa. Many Americans felt that perhaps now was the time for the United States to join with its ally, Great Britain and stop the Axis from taking over more regions of the world.

In 1941, Franklin Roosevelt was President of the United States. His fear at the time was that Japan would try to take over many countries in Asia. He did not want to see that happen, so he moved some of the United States warships that had been stationed in San Diego, to the military base at Pearl Harbor, in Honolulu, Hawaii.

Japan quietly plotted their attack. They waited until the early hours of the morning on Sunday, December 7, 1941. Then, 350 Japanese war plans began to drop bombs on the U.S. ships at Pearl Harbor. The first bombs fell at 7:48 am and a mere 90 minutes later, the attack was over. Pearl Harbor was decimated. 8 battleships were damaged. Eleven ships were sunk and 300 U.S. planes were destroyed. Most devastating was the loss of life 2,400 U.S. military members was killed in the attack and 1,282 were injured.

President Roosevelt addressed the country via the radio and said "Today is a day that will live in infamy." He asked Congress to declare war on Japan. War was declared on Japan on December 8th and on Germany and Italy on December 11th. The United States had entered World War Two.

29. After reading the passage, what can we infer infamy means?

   a. Famous
   b. Remembered in a good way
   c. Remembered in a bad way
   d. Easily forgotten

30. What three countries formed the Axis?

   a. Italy, England, Germany
   b. United States, England, Italy
   c. Germany, Japan, Italy
   d. Germany, Japan, United States

31. What do you think was President Roosevelt's reason for moving warships to Pearl Harbor?

   a. He feared Japan would bomb San Diego
   b. He knew Japan was going to attack Pearl Harbor
   c. He was planning to attack Japan
   d. He wanted to try to protect Asian countries from Japanese takeover

32. Why do you think Japan chose a Sunday morning at 7:48 am for their attack?

   a. They knew the military slept late
   b. There is a law against bombing countries on a Sunday
   c. They wanted the attack to catch people by surprise
   d. That was the only free time they had to attack.

Questions 33 - 36 refer to the following passage.

Passage 7 - The Circulatory System

The circulatory system is an organ system that passes nutrients (such as amino acids and electrolytes), gases, hormones, and blood cells to and from cells in the body to help fight diseases and help stabilize body temperature and pH levels.

The circulatory system may be seen strictly as a blood distribution network, but some consider the circulatory system as composed of the cardiovascular system, which distributes blood, and the lymphatic system, which distributes lymph. While humans, as well as other vertebrates, have a closed cardiovascular system (meaning that the blood never leaves the network of arteries, veins and capillaries), some invertebrate groups have an open cardiovascular system. The most primitive animal phyla lack circulatory systems. The lymphatic system, on the other hand, is an open system.

Two types of fluids move through the circulatory system: blood and lymph. The blood, heart, and blood vessels form the cardiovascular system. The lymph, the lymph nodes, and lymph vessels form the lymphatic system. The cardiovascular system and the lymphatic system collectively make up the circulatory system.

The main components of the human cardiovascular system are the heart and the blood vessels. It includes: the pulmonary circulation, a "loop" through the lungs where blood is oxygenated; and the systemic circulation, a "loop" through the rest of the body to provide oxygenated blood. An average adult contains five to six quarts (roughly 4.7 to 5.7 liters) of blood, which consists of plasma, red blood cells, white blood cells, and platelets. Also, the digestive system works with the circulatory system to provide the nutrients the system needs to keep the heart pumping.

http://en.wikipedia.org/wiki/Circulatory_System.

33. What can we infer from the first paragraph?

    a. An important purpose of the circulatory system is that of fighting diseases.

    b. The most important function of the circulatory system is to give the person energy.

    c. The least important function of the circulatory system is that of growing skin cells.

    d. The entire purpose of the circulatory system is not known.

34. Do humans have an open or closed circulatory system?

    a. Open
    b. Closed
    c. Usually open, though sometimes closed
    d. Usually closed, though sometimes open

35. In addition to blood, what two components form the cardiovascular system?

    a. The heart and the lungs
    b. The lungs and the veins
    c. The heart and the blood vessels
    d. The blood vessels and the nerves

36. Which system, along with the circulatory system, helps provide nutrients to keep the human heart pumping?

   a. The skeletal system

   b. The digestive system

   c. The immune system

   d. The nervous system

Questions 37 - 40 refer to the following passage.

Passage 8 FDR, the Treaty of Versailles, and the Fourteen Points

At the conclusion of World War I, both those who had won the war and those who were forced to admit defeat welcomed the end of the war and anticipated that a peace treaty would be signed. The American president, Franklin D. Roosevelt, played an important part in proposing what the agreements should be and did so through his Fourteen Points.

World War I had begun in 1914 when an Austrian archduke was assassinated, leading to a domino effect that pulled the world's most powerful countries into war on a large scale. The war catalyzed the creation and use of deadly weapons that had not previously existed, resulting in a great loss of soldiers on both sides of the fighting. More than 9 million soldiers were killed.

The United States agreed to enter the war right before it ended, and they believed that its decision to become finally involved brought on the end of the war. FDR made it very clear that the U.S. was entering the war for moral reasons and had an agenda focused on world peace. The Fourteen Points were individual goals and ideas (focused on peace, free trade, open communication, and self reliance) that FDR wanted the power nations to strive for now that the war had concluded. He was optimistic and had many ideas about what could be accomplished through and during the post-war peace. However, FDR's fourteen points were poorly received when he presented them to the leaders of other world powers, many of whom wanted only to help their own countries and to punish the Germans for fueling the war, and they fell by the wayside. World War II was imminent, for Germany lost everything.

Some historians believe that the other leaders who participated in the Treaty of Versailles weren't receptive to the Fourteen Points because World War I was fought almost entirely on European soil, and the United States lost much less than did the other powers. FDR was in a unique position to determine the fate of the war, but doing it on his own terms did not help accomplish his goals. This is only one historical example of how the United State has tried to use its power as an important country, but found itself limited because of geological or ideological factors.

37. The main idea of this passage is that

a. World War I was unfair because no fighting took place in America.

b. World War II happened because of the Treaty of Versailles.

c. the power the United States has to help other countries also prevents it from helping other countries.

d. Franklin D. Roosevelt was one of the United States' smartest presidents.

38. According to the second paragraph, World War I started because

a. an archduke was assassinated.

b. weapons that were more deadly had been developed.

c. a domino effect of allies agreeing to help each other.

d. the world's most powerful countries were large.

39. The author includes the detail that 9 million soldiers were killed

a. to demonstrate why European leaders were hesitant to accept peace.

b. to show the reader the dangers of deadly weapons.

c. to make the reader think about which countries lost the most soldiers.

d. to demonstrate why World War II was imminent.

40. According to this passage, the word catalyzed means

a. analyzed
b. sped up
c. invented
d. funded

Section IV – Math

1. The sum of the digits of a 2-digit number is 12. If we switch the digits, the number we get will be greater than the initial one by 36. Find the initial number.

   a. 39
   b. 48
   c. 57
   d. 75

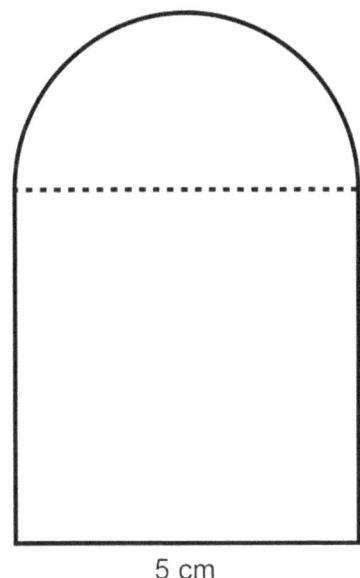

5 cm

Note: figure not drawn to scale

2. What is the perimeter of the above shape?

   a. 17.5 π cm
   b. 20 π cm
   c. 15 π cm
   d. 25 π cm

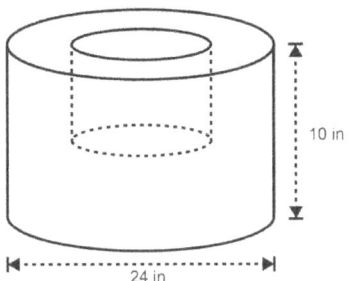

Note: figure not drawn to scale

3. What is the volume of the above solid made by a hollow cylinder that is half the size (in all dimensions) of the larger cylinder?

   a. 1440 π in³
   b. 1260 π in³
   c. 1040 π in³
   d. 960 π in³

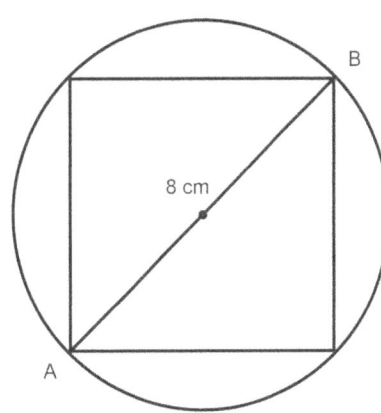

Note: figure not drawn to scale

4. What is area of the circle?

   a. 4 π cm²
   b. 12 π cm²
   c. 10 π cm²
   d. 16 π cm²

5. John jogs around a 75-meter diameter track 7 times. How much linear distance did he cover?

   a. 1250 meters
   b. 1450 meters
   c. 1650 meters
   d. 1725 meters

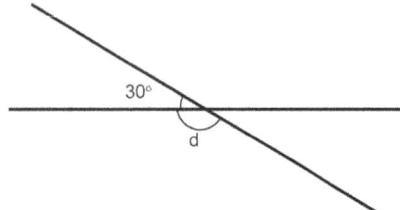

6. What is the indicated angle above?

   a. 150°
   b. 330°
   c. 60°
   d. 120°

7. On a circular jogging track with a circumference of 1.2 km, John, Tony and David walk at the rate of 120, 100 and 75 meters per minute respectively. If they all start walking in the same direction, how long will it take until they are together again?

   a. 200 minutes
   b. 220 minutes
   c. 240 minutes
   d. 260 minutes

8. On a scaled map, city A is 12.4 cm away from city B. If the scale is 1 cm = 5 km then what is the actual distance between these two cities?

   a. 12.4 km
   b. 48.4 km
   c. 58 km
   d. 62 km

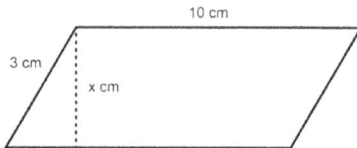

9. What is the perimeter of the parallelogram above?

   a. 12 cm
   b. 26 cm
   c. 13 cm
   d. (13+x) cm

10. Estimate 2009 x 108.

   a. 110,000
   b. 2,0000
   c. 21,000
   d. 210,000

11. The playing times for three songs on a compact disc are as follows: 4 minutes 56 seconds for song A, 2 minutes 30 seconds for song B, 10 minutes 16 seconds for song C. What is the average playing time for the three songs?

   a. 17 minutes 42 seconds
   b. 6 minutes 7 seconds
   c. 6 minutes
   d. 5 minutes 54 seconds

12. John is a barber and receives 40% of the amount paid by his customers, and all of the tips. If a customer pays $8.50 for a haircut and leaves a tip of $1.30, how much money does John receive?

   a. $3.92
   b. $4.70
   c. $5.30
   d. $6.40

13. The length of a rectangle is 5 in. more than its width. The perimeter of the rectangle is 26 in. What is the width and length of the rectangle?

   a. Width 6 in., Length 9 in.
   b. Width 4 in., Length 9 in.
   c. Width 4 in., Length 5 in.
   d. Width 6 in., Length 11 in.

14. Calculate (3a + 4b) * d when A = 2, b = 4 and d = 8

   a. 40
   b. 150
   c. 112
   d. 176

15. c = 4, n = 5 and x = 3. Calculate 2cnx/2n

   a. 12
   b. 50
   c. 8
   d. 21

16. Simplify 3 1/2 / 2 4/5

   a. 1 1/4
   b. 2 1/4
   c. 1 1/3
   d. 2 1/3

17. Solve 2b/3 + 3a/5 – 2, where b = 9 and a = 10

   a. 5
   b. 10
   c. 20
   d. 9

18. Simplify (1/3 + 2/6) - (3/4 - 1/3)

   a. 1/4
   b. 5/11
   c. 3/7
   d. 2/9

19. Simplify (4/5 - 3/10) + (2/3 – 3/9) =

   a. 4/11
   b. 2/15
   c. 7/15
   d. 9/11

20. Translate the following into an equation: 2 + a number divided by 7.

   a. (2 + X)/7
   b. (7 + X)/2
   c. (2 + 7)/X
   d. 2/(7 + X)

21. If a = 12 and b = 8, solve 6b - a + 2a

   a. 12/9
   b. 18
   c. 16
   d. 12

22. Simplify 3 2/3 - 1 2/8

   a. 3/5
   b. 3/5
   c. 2 5/12
   d. 1 5/12

23. Simplify 7 2/5 – 4 3/10

   a. 3 1/10
   b. 3 2/5
   c. 4 1/5
   d. 3 7/10

24. Solve for x. -4 – 5x = 8x + 8

   a. 6
   b. 3
   c. 4
   d. 2

25. Solve 2 1/3 x 1 3/7 x 3/4

   a. 2 1/2
   b. 9
   c. 3 2/3
   d. 2 2/5

26. Simplify 7 4/5 – 4 2/3

   a. 4 2/5
   b. 3 2/15
   c. 3 7/15
   d. 4 3/5

27. Solve for x. 12x - 8 = 3x + 10

   a. 6
   b. 4
   c. 2
   d. 3

28. Simplify (3/5 - 2/5) + (3/4 – 2/8)

   a. 18/45
   b. 7/11
   c. 18/40
   d. 12/19

29. Solve for a. 6a + 4 = 28 + 2a

   a. 4
   b. 8
   c. 2
   d. 6

30. Simplify (3/4 - 1/4) - (3/5 – 2/5)

   a. 9/20
   b. 4/15
   c. 7/15
   d. 11/20

31. Solve for x. 6 + 9x = 12 + 7x

   a. 5
   b. 2
   c. 4
   d. 3

32. Simplify 6 2/5 / 2 2/7

   a. 2 1/4
   b. 1 1/5
   c. 2 4/5
   d. 2 2/3

33. Solve for a. -6 + 7a = 9 + 4a

   a. 3
   b. 5
   c. 2
   d. 6

34. A square lawn has an area of 62,500 square meters. What is the cost of building fence around it at a rate of $5.5 per meter?

   a. $4000
   b. $4500
   c. $5000
   d. $5500

35. The following numbers are the ages of people on a bus – 3, 6, 27, 13, 6, 8, 12, 20, 5, 10. Calculate their average of their ages.

   a. 11
   b. 6
   c. 9
   d. 110

36. A farmer wants to plant 65,536 trees in such a way that number of rows must be equal to the number of plants in a row. How many trees will he plant in a row?

   a. 1684
   b. 1268
   c. 668
   d. 256

37. How much pay does Mr. Johnson receive if he gives half of his pay to his family, $250 to his landlord, and has exactly 3/7 of his pay left after these expenses?

   a. $3600
   b. $3500
   c. $2800
   d. $1750

38. A boy has 4 red, 5 green and 2 yellow balls. He chooses two balls randomly. What is the probability that one is red and other is green?

   a. 2/11
   b. 19/22
   c. 20/121
   d. 9/11

39. Simplify 5 1/2 – 5 3/7

   a. 1/10
   b. 1/14
   c. 1/7
   d. 2/7

40. What is -3 - (-7) - (+5)?

   a. -6
   b. 6
   c. 3
   d. -1

41. Solve 3 3/4 x 4/5 x 1 3/4

   a. 3 3/4
   b. 4 1/3
   c. 6
   d. 5 1/4

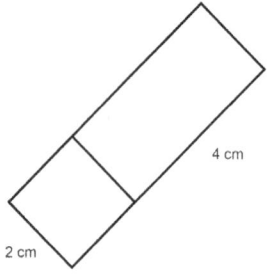

Note: figure not drawn to scale

42. Assuming the shape with a 2cm. side is square, what is the perimeter of the above shape?

    a. 12 cm
    b. 16 cm
    c. 6 cm
    d. 20 cm

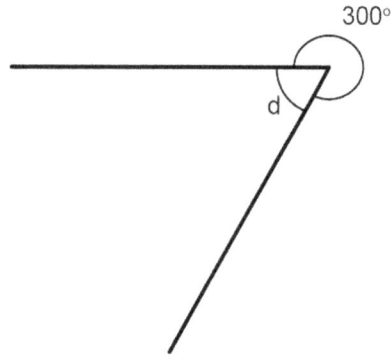

43. What is the measurement of the indicated angle?

    a. 45°
    b. 90°
    c. 60°
    d. 50°

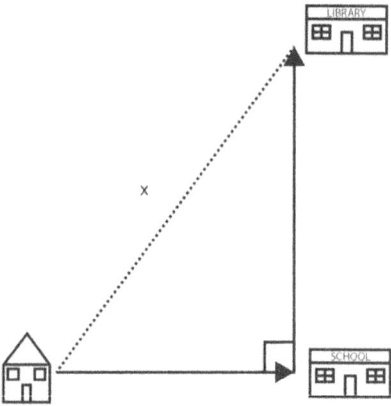

44. Every day starting from his home Peter travels due east 3 kilometers to the school. After school he travels due north 4 kilometers to the library. What is the distance between Peter's home and the library?

    a. 15 km
    b. 10 km
    c. 5 km
    d. 12 ½ km

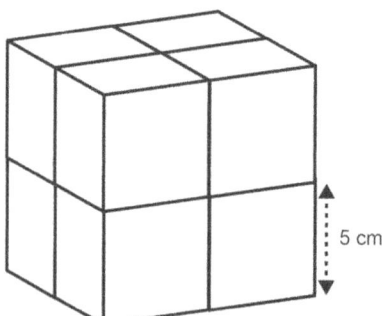

45. What is the volume of the figure above?

    a. 125 cm^3
    b. 875 cm^3
    c. 1000 cm^3
    d. 500 cm^3

Answer Key

Section I Verbal Reasoning

1. B
Able and competent are synonyms.

2. A
Antidote and cure are synonyms.

3. C
Consensus and agreement are synonyms.

4. A
Magnify and amplify are synonyms.

5. B
Immaculate and perfect are synonyms.

6. C
Feasible and viable are synonyms.

7. B
Reason and rationale are synonyms.

8. A
Tinge and touch are synonyms.

9. C
Gist and summary are synonyms.

10. C
Initiate and instigate are synonyms.

11. A
Expertise and specialty are synonyms.

12. A
Fertile and fruitful are synonyms.

13. A
Rowdy and noisy are synonyms.

14. A
Courteous and polite are synonyms.

15. A
Lean and thin are synonyms.

16. B
Audacious and daring are synonyms.

17. A
Constitute and establish are synonyms.

18. A
Corrupt and unscrupulous are synonyms.

19. A
Dispense and distribute are synonyms.

20. B
Duration and length are synonyms.

21. B
Her talent was <u>extraordinary</u> (very unusual or remarkable) and so it wowed the audience.

22. C
Jean was <u>angry</u> when her little brother destroyed her favorite doll.

23. A
We will <u>ask</u> about our scores on the pop quiz.

24. A
The car accident was a <u>terrible</u> experience the victims want to forget.

25. C
Cinderella's <u>evil</u> (or commonly, wicked) stepmother failed in the end.

26. B
Her business success showed that she was very <u>astute</u> (having or showing an ability to accurately assess situations or people and turn this to one's advantage).

27. A
It is boring and I would rather not go, but the ceremony is mandatory (compulsory).

28. C
We don't want to hear the whole thing. Just the relevant (closely connected or appropriate to the matter at hand) facts please.

29. A
She works in a cubicle answering the phone all day. Her doctor says she is too sedentary (tending to spend much time seated; somewhat inactive).

30. B
I don't know why he is being so nice. I am sure he has an ulterior (beyond what is obvious or admitted) motive.

31. A
We cannot reveal the source. It was posted by anonymous (not identified by name; of unknown name).

32. C
I have never seen anyone so rude. His behavior was atrocious (wicked, horrifying)

33. B
I see that sign everywhere. It is much more prevalent (widespread) than I thought.

34. B
Her attitude was very nonchalant (casually calm and relaxed).

35. A
The water in the pond has been sitting for so long it is stagnant (lacking freshness, motion, flow, progress, or change; stale; motionless; still).

36. D
I cannot wait to try some of the delicious dishes served in the new restaurant.

37. B
Can you describe the character of Juliet in the play?

38. A
The soldiers ruined the rebel's camp. It is possible the soldiers could have fixed the rebel's camp, but generally soldiers and rebels are opposed, so 'ruined' is the best answer.

39. B
There is a big dissimilarity (difference) in Esther and Pete's grades. Since the comparison is between two students, choice B is the only one that makes sense.

40. D
I can achieve (attain) my goals in life when I study hard.

Section II – Quantitative Reasoning

1. A
(6 - 4) (3/5 – 4/5) = 2 (3 - 4/5) = since 3 is less than 4, we would have to subtract 1 from the whole number besides the fraction, therefore 1 13 - 4/5 = 1 9/5 = 2 4/5

2. B
46,227 + 101,032 = 147.259, or about 147,000.

3. A
$\sqrt{121} = 11$

4. B
Let the father's age = Y, and Kate's age = X, therefore Y = 32 + X, in 5 years y = 5x, substituting for Y will be 5x = 32 + X, 5x – x = 32, 4X = 32, X = 32/8, x = 8, Kate will be 8 in 5 years time, so Kate's present age = 8 - 5 = 3.

5. A

If she can type a full page in p minutes, then in 5 minutes she can type 5/p.

6. A

This is an inverse ratio problem.

1/x = 1/a + 1/b where a is the time Sally can paint a house, b is the time John can paint a house, x is the time Sally and John can together paint a house.

So,

1/x = 1/4 + 1/6 ... We use the least common multiple in the denominator that is 24:

1/x = 6/24 + 4/24

1/x = 10/24

x = 24/10

x = 2.4 hours.

In other words; 2 hours + 0.4 hours = 2 hours + 0.4•60 minutes

= 2 hours 24 minutes

7. B

Last season's ticket = X, 110%X = 880 tickets, %X = 880/110, 100%X = 880/110 x 100 = 800

8. B

This is an inverse proportion question. The number of employees decreases then working time will increase.

Employees   Working hours

12   7
10   x

Therefore, the equation will be x/7 = 12/10

x = 7 * 12/10

x = 7.2

Therefore, the remaining staff will have to work, in minutes, 0.2 × 60 = 12 minutes.

9. B

The speed is 300km/hr so it will cover 5 km/minute. Therefore, the train will travel 45km in 9 minutes. Time to arrive at station B will be 8:56 + 9 = 9:05 pm.

10. B

Suppose oranges in the basket before = x
Then according to the condition
X + 8x/5 = 130
5x + 8x = 650
X = 50

11. C

Number of problems remaining = 40 – 28 = 12
Time remaining = 30 – 25 = 5 minutes = 5 X 60 = 300 seconds. Time for each remaining question = 300/12 = 25 seconds.

12. B

2/3Z + 10 = 3 X 15
2/3 Z = 45 – 10
Z = 35 X 3/2
Z = 52.5

13. A

1/3 X 27 = 9 + 25 = 34

14. A

The purchase price of 12 shirts when profit is 8% = 0.92 X 336 = $309.
The purchase price of each shirt = 309/12 = $25.75

15. C

This is a proportionality question.
12 : 4
X : 20

4 * 5 = 20 and 12 * 5 = X
X = 60

16. C
Z = (5 X 5) – 10
Z = 15

17. A
2/3 of 100 = 66.66 X 5 = 333.33

18. B
.97 - .49 = .48
.76 + .21 = .97

19. B
1/3 + 1/5 + 3/6 = 10/30 + 6/30 + 15/30 = 31/30
2/3 + ¾ = 8/12 + 9/12 = 17/12

20. A
2/8 + 5/6 = 6/24 + 20/24 = 26/24
6/8 + 4/2 = 6/8 + 16/8 = 22/8

21. B
1800 X 16% = 288

22. A
The area of a square with 5 cm sides will be 5 X 5 = 25 cm²
The area of a rectangle with 2 cm and 10 cm sides will be 2 X 10 = 20 cm²

23. A
Area of the circle = A = ∏ X r2 A = 3.14 X 192 = 1133.54
Area of the square = 25 X 25 = 625

24. A
Area of the circle = A = ∏ X r2 A = 3.14 X 92 = 254.34
Area of the triangle = ½ (B*H) = (5 X 10) / 2 = 25

25. A
40% of 500 = 200
12% of 1350 = 162

26. B
22% of 60 = 132
18% of 150 = 27

27. B
15% of 50 = 7.5
12% of 75 = 9

28. A
.234 + .673 = .907
.990 - .378 = .612

29. A
Probability of drawing a red ball = 6/10
Probability of drawing a yellow ball = 4/10

30. A
Probability of drawing a red ball = 6/15
Probability of drawing a green ball = 4/15

31. B
75 X 22% = 16.5 so the cost is 75 – 16.5 = $58.50
100 X 35% = 35 so the cost is 100 – 35 = $65

32. B
.993 - .34 = .653
2/5 = .4

33. A
1/3 + 4/7 = 7/21 + 12/21 = 19/21 = .9047
6.93 - 6.34 = .59

34. A
.25 + .67 = 0.92
.89 - .34 = 0.55

35. A
.13 + .64 = .77
.62 - .14 = .48

Section III –
Reading Comprehension

1. B
We can infer an important part of the respiratory system are the lungs. From the passage, "Molecules of oxygen and carbon dioxide are passively exchanged, by diffusion, between the gaseous external environment and the blood. This exchange process occurs in the alveolar region of the lungs."

Therefore, one primary function for the respiratory system is the exchange of oxygen and carbon dioxide, and this process occurs in the lungs. We can therefore infer that the lungs are an important part of the respiratory system.

2. C
The process by which molecules of oxygen and carbon dioxide are passively exchanged is diffusion.

This is a definition type question. Scan the passage for references to "oxygen," "carbon dioxide," or "exchanged."

3. A
The organ that plays an important role in gas exchange in amphibians is the skin.

Scan the passage for references to "amphibians," and find the answer.

4. A
The three physiological zones of the respiratory system are Conducting, transitional, respiratory zones.

5. B
This warranty does not cover a product that you have tried to fix yourself. From paragraph two, "This limited warranty does not cover … any unauthorized disassembly, repair, or modification. "

6. C
ABC Electric could either replace or repair the fan, provided the other conditions are met. ABC Electric has the option to repair or replace.

7. B
The warranty does not cover a stove damaged in a flood. From the passage, "This limited warranty does not cover any damage to the product from improper installation, accident, abuse, misuse, natural disaster, insufficient or excessive electrical supply, abnormal mechanical or environmental conditions."

A flood is an "abnormal environmental condition," and a natural disaster, so it is not covered.

8. A
A missing part is an example of defective workmanship. This is an error made in the manufacturing process. A defective part is not considered workmanship.

9. B
The first paragraph tells us that myths are a true account of the remote past.

The second paragraph tells us that, "myths generally take place during a primordial age, when the world was still young, before achieving its current form."

Putting these two together, we can infer that humankind used myth to explain how the world was created.

10. A
This passage is about different types of stories. First, the passage explains myths, and then compares other types of stories to myths.

11. B
From the passage, "Unlike myths, folktales can take place at any time and any place, and the natives do not usually consider them true or sacred."

12. A
Based on the partial table of contents, this book is most likely about how to answer multiple choice.

13. B
This passage describes the different categories for traditional stories. The other options are facts from the passage, not the main idea of the passage. The main idea of a passage will always be the most general statement. For example, choice A, Myths, fables, and folktales are not the same thing, and each describes a specific type of story. This is a true statement from the passage, but not the main idea of the passage, since the passage also talks about how some cultures may classify a story as a myth and others as a folktale.

The statement, from choice B, Traditional stories can be categorized in different ways by different people, is a more general statement that describes the passage.

14. B
Choice B is the best choice, categories that group traditional stories according to certain characteristics.

Choices A and C are false and can be eliminated right away. Choice D is designed to confuse. Choice D may be true, but it is not mentioned in the passage.

15. D
The best answer is choice D, traditional stories themselves are a part of the larger category of folklore, which may also include costumes, gestures, and music.

All the other choices are false. Traditional stories are part of the larger category of Folklore, which includes other things, not the other way around.

16. A
There is a distinct difference between a myth and a legend, although both are folktales.

17. A
Choice A is a re-wording of text from the passage.

18. C
This is taken directly from the passage.

19. C
Although trees are used as a building material, this is not their primary use. Trees are a primary energy source.

20. A
This is taken directly from the passage.

21. D
This question is designed to confuse by presenting different choices for the two chemicals, oxygen and carbon dioxide. One is produced, and one is reduced. Read the passage carefully to see which is reduced and which is produced.

22. D
This question tests the reader's summarization skills. The other answers A, B, and C focus on portions of the second paragraph that are too narrow and do not relate to the specific portion of text in question. The complexity of the sentence may mislead students into selecting one of these answers, but rearranging or restating the sentence will lead the reader to the correct answer. In addition, A makes an assumption that may or may not be true about the intentions of the company, B focuses on one product rather than the idea of the products, and C makes an assumption about women that may or may not be true and is not supported by the text.

23. B
This question tests reader's attention to detail. If a reader selects A, he or she may have picked up on the use of the word "debate" and assumed, very logically, that the two are at odds because they are fighting; however, this is simply not supported in the text. C also uses very specific quotes from the text, but it rearranges them and gives them false meaning. The artists want to elevate their creations above the creations of other artists, thereby showing that they are "creative" and "innovative." Similarly, D takes phrases straight from the texts and rearranges and confuses them. The artists are described as wanting to be "creative, innovative, individual people," not the women.

24. A
This question tests reader's vocabulary and summarization skills. This phrase, used by the author, may seem flippant and dismissive if readers focus on the word "whatever" and misinterpret it as a popular, colloquial terms. In this way, the answers B and C may mislead the reader to selecting one of them

by including the terms "unimportant" and "stupid," respectively. D is a similar misreading, but doesn't make sense when the phrase is at the beginning of the passage and the entire passage is on media messages. A is literally and contextually appropriate, and the reader can understand that the author would like to keep the introduction focused on the topic the passage is going to discuss.

25. A
This question tests a reader's inference skills. The extreme use of the word "all" in B suggests that every single advertising company are working to be approachable, and while this is not only unlikely, the text specifically states that "more" companies have done this, signifying that they have not all participated, even if it's a possibility that they may some day. The use of the limiting word "only" in C lends that answer similar problems; women are still buying from companies who do not care about this message, or those companies would not be in business, and the passage specifies that "many" women are worried about media messages, but not all. Readers may find D logical, especially if they are looking to make an inference, and while this may be a possibility, the passage does not suggest or discuss this happening. A is correct based on specifically because of the relation between "still working" in the answer and "will hopefully" and the extensive discussion on companies struggles, which come only with progress, in the text.

26. B
The time limit for radar detectors is 14 days. Since you made the purchase 15 days ago, you do not qualify for the guarantee.

27. B
Since you made the purchase 10 days ago, you are covered by the guarantee. Since it is an advertised price at a different store, ABC Electric will "beat" the price by 10% of the difference, which is,

500 – 400 = 100 – difference in price

100 X 10% = $10 – 10% of the difference

The advertised lower price is $400. ABC will beat this price by 10% so they will refund $100 + 10 = $110.

28. C
The purpose of this passage is to persuade.

29. C
To be infamous means to be remembered for an evil or terrible action. Therefore, the word infamy means to remember a bad or terrible thing. Choice A is incorrect because being famous is not the same as being infamous. Choice B is incorrect because the attack on Pearl Harbor was not good. Choice D is incorrect because Pearl Harbor was not forgotten.

30. C
Each answer choice except choice C contains the name of at least one country that was not part of the AXIS powers.

31. D
It is stated in the passage. Choice A is not correct because there was no indication that Japan would attack San Diego. Choice B is incorrect because the attack on Pearl Harbor was a surprise. Choice C is incorrect because Roosevelt was not planning to attack Japan.

32. C
The passage clearly states that Japan planned a surprise attack. They chose that early time to catch the U.S. military off guard. Choice A is incorrect because the military does not sleep late. Choice B is incorrect because there is no law against bombing countries. Choice D is incorrect because it makes no sense.

33. A
We can infer that an important purpose of the circulatory system is that of fighting diseases.

34. B
Humans have a closed circulatory system.

35. C
Besides blood, the heart and the blood vessels form the cardiovascular system.

36. B
The digestive system, along with the circulatory system, helps provide nutrients to keep the human heart pumping.

37. C
This question tests the reader's summarization skills. The entire passage is leading up to the idea that the president of the US may not have had grounds to assert his Fourteen Points when other countries had lost so much. A is pretty directly inferred by the text, but it does not adequately summarize what the entire passage is trying to communicate. B may also be inferred by the passage when it says that the war is "imminent," but it does not represent the entire message, either. The passage does seem to be in praise of FDR, or at least in respect of him, but it does not in any way claim that he is the smartest president, nor does this represent the many other points included. C is then the obvious answer, and most directly relates to the closing sentences which it rewords.

38. C
This question tests the reader's attention to detail. The passage does state that A and B are true, and while those statements are in proximity to the explanation for why the war started, they are not the reasons given. D is a mix up of words used in the passage, which says that the largest powers were in

play but not that this fact somehow started the war. The passage does make a direct statement that a domino effect started the war, supporting C as the correct answer.

39. A
This question tests the reader's understanding of functions in writing. Throughout the passage, it states that leaders of other nations were hesitant to accept generous or peaceful terms because of the grievances of the war, and the great loss of life was chief among these. While the passage does touch on the devastation of deadly weapons (B), the use of this raw, emotional fact serves a larger purpose, and the focus of the passage is not weapons. While readers may indeed consider who lost the most soldiers (C) when many countries were involved and the inequalities of loss are mentioned in the passage, there is no discussion of this in the passage. D is related to A, But A is more direct and relates more to the passage.

40. B
This question tests the reader's vocabulary skills. A may seem appealing to readers because it is phonetically similar to "catalyzed," but the two are not related in any other way. C makes sense in context, but if plugged in to the sentence creates a redundancy that doesn't make sense. D does also not make sense contextually, even if the reader may consider that funds were needed to create more weaponry, especially if it was advanced.

Section V – Math

1. B
Let XY represent the initial number, X + Y = 12, YX=XY+ 36, only b = 48 satisfies both equations.

2. A
The problem is to find the perimeter of a shape made by merging a square and a semi circle. Perimeter = 3 sides of the square + 1/2 circumference of the circle.
= (3 × 5) + ½(5 π)
= 15 + 2.5 π
Perimeter = 17.5 π cm

3. B
Volume = Volume of large cylinder - Volume of small cylinder
(Volume of cylinder = area of base × height)
Volume = (π 12^2× 10) - (π 6^2× 5),
1440π - 180π
Volume = 1260π in^3

4. D
We have a circle given with diameter 8 cm and a square located within the circle. We are asked to find the area of the circle for which we only need to know the length of the radius that is the half of the diameter.

Area of circle = πr^2 ... r = 8/2 = 4 cm

Area of circle = π•4^2

= 16π cm^2 ... As we notice, the inner square has no role in this question.

5. C
In one trip around the track, he covers the distance equal to the circumference of the circular path.
Circumference of the path = 75 × π = 235.65 meters.
Distance covered in 7 times around = 235.65 × 7 = 1650 meters.

6. A
The angles opposite both angles 30° & angle d are respectively equal to vertical angles.
2(30° + d) = 360°
2d = 360° - 60°
2d = 300°
d = 150°

7. C
The length of the track = 1.2 km = 1200 meters.
John will complete 1 round in 1200/120 = 10 minutes.
Tony will complete 1 round in 1200/100 = 12 minutes.
David will complete 1 round in 1200/75 = 16 minutes.
The Least Common Multiple of these is 240. Therefore, they will be together after 240 minutes.

8. D
1 cm = 5 km so 12.4 cm will be = 12.4 × 5 = 62 km.

9. B
Perimeter of a parallelogram is the sum of the sides.

Perimeter = 2(l+b)
Perimeter = 2(3+10), 2 × 13
Perimeter = 26 cm

10. D
2009 X 108 is approximately 210,000. The actual number is 216,972.

11. D
First, convert everything to seconds.
Song A = 240 + 56 = 296 sec.
Song B = 120 + 30 = 150 sec.
Song C = 600 + 16 = 616 sec.
Total = 296 + 150 + 616 = 1062. Average will be 1062/3 = 354.
In hours, 354/60 = 5 minutes, 54 seconds.

12. B
8.50 * .4 = 3.40 + 1.30 = $4.70

13. B
Formula for perimeter of a rectangle is 2(L + W)
p=26, so 2(L+W) = p

The length is 5 inches more than the width, so
2(w+5) + 2w = 26
2w + 10 + 2w = 26
2w + 2w = 26 - 10
4w = 18
W = 16/4 = 4 inches
L is 5 inches more than w, so
L = 5 + 4 = 9 inches.

14. D
Substitute the known variables, (3 x 2) + (4 x 4) x 8 =, 6 + 16 x 8, 24 x 8 = 176

15. A
2cnx = 2(4 x 5 x 3)/(2 X 5) = (2 x 60)/(2 x 5) = 120/10 = 12

16. A
First change all the terms to fractions, therefore, we get 7/2 / 14/5, to divide we need to invert the second fraction, 7/2 x 5/14, and then we cancel out to reduce to the lowest terms, 1/2 x 5/2 = 5/4, convert back to proper fraction to get 1 1/4

17. B
Substitute known variables, 2 x 9/3 + 3 x 10/5 - 2 =, 18/3 + 30/5 - 2 =, 6 + 6 -2 =, 12 - 2 = 10

18. A
First solve the fraction in each bracket separately, therefore (1/3 + 2/6) - (3/4 - 1/3) = (find common denominator) (2+2/6) - (9- 4/12) = (4/6) - (5/12) = (find common denominator again) 2/3 - 5/12 =, 8 - 5/12 = 3/12 = 1/4.

19. B
(4/5 - 3/10) + (2/3 – 3/9) =, (find a common denominator) (8-3/10) + (6-3/9) =, (5/10) + (3/9) = 2/5 + 1/3, (find a common denominator) 6+5/15 = 11/15

20. A
2 + a number divided by 7.
(2 + X) divided by 7.
(2 + X)/7

21. D
Substitute with known variables, (6 x 8) – 12 + (2 x 12) =, 48 – 12 + 24, do the additions first, 48 – (12 + 24) =, 48 – 36 = 12

22. C
Subtract the whole numbers and then subtract the fractions, therefore 3 2/3 - 1 2/8 = (3-1) (2/3 – 2/8) = find common denominator to subtract the fractions, (2) (16-6)/24 = 2 10/24, reduce to lowest terms, 2 5/12

23. A
Subtract the whole numbers and then subtract the fractions, therefore (7-4) (2/5 – 3/10) = 3 (4-3/10) = 3 1/10

24. C
-4 – 5x = 8x + 8, bring same terms to same side of the equation changing the negative or positive signs when they cross over, therefore -5x +8x = 8 + 4, = 3x = 12, x = 12/3 = 4.

25. A
First, convert all the terms to fractions and then cancel out. Therefore, 7/3 x 10/7 x 3/4 = 1/3 x 10/1 x 3/4, 1 x 5 x 1/2, 5 x 1/2 = 2 1/2

26. B
Subtract the whole numbers and then subtract the fractions, therefore (7 - 4) (4/5 – 2/3) = 3 (12 - 10/15) = 3 2/15

27. C
12x – 8 = 3x + 10, bring same terms to same side of the equation changing the negative or positive signs when they cross over, therefore 12x -3x = 10 + 8, 9x = 18, x = 2

28. C
(3/5 - 2/5) + (3/4 – 2/8) =, (3-2/5) + (6 - 2/8) =, 1/5 + 4/8 =, (find a common denominator) 8+10/40 = 18/40

29. D
6a + 4 = 28 + 2a, solve for a. Bring same terms to same side of the equation changing the negative or positive signs when they cross over, therefore 6a – 2a = 28 - 4, 4a = 24, a = 24/4 = 6

30. D
(3-1/4) – (3-2/5) =, 3/4 - 1/5 =. 15-4/20 = 11/20

31. D
6 + 9x = 12 + 7x, bring same terms to same side of the equation changing the negative or positive signs when they cross over, therefore 9x – 7x = 12 – 6, 2x = 6, x = 6/2, x = 3

32. C
First change all the terms to fractions, therefore, we get 32/5 / 16/7, to divide we need to invert the second fraction, 32/5 x 7/16, and then we cancel out to reduce to the lowest terms, 2/5 x 7/1 = 14/5, convert back to proper fraction to get 2 4/5

33. B
-6 + 7a = 9 + 4a, bring same terms to same side of the equation changing the negative or positive signs when they cross over, therefore 7a – 4a = 9 + 6 = 3a = 15, a = 15/3, a = 5

34. D
As the lawn is square, the length of one side will be= $\sqrt{62500}$ = 250 meters. Therefore, the perimeters will be 250 × 4 = 1000 meters. The total cost will be 1000 × 5.5 = $5500.

35. A
First add all the numbers 3 + 6 + 27 + 13 + 6 + 8 + 12 + 20 + 5 + 10 = 110. Then divide by 10 (the number of data provided) = 110/10 = 11

36. D
Let x be number of rows, and number of trees in a row. So equation becomes X^2 = 65536, X = 256.

37. B
We check the fractions in the question and see that there is a "half" (that is 1/2) and 3/7. So, we multiply the denominators of these fractions to decide how to name the total money. We say that Mr. Johnson has 14x at the beginning; he gives half of this, meaning 7x, to his family. $250 to his landlord. He has 3/7 of his money left. 3/7 of 14x is equal to:

14x•(3/7) = 6x

So,

Spent money is: 7x + 250

Unspent money is: 6x

Total money is: 14x

We write an equation: total money = spent money + unspent money

14x = 7x + 250 + 6x

14x - 7x - 6x = 250

x = 250

We are asked to find the total money that is 14x:

14x = 14•250 = $3500

38. A
The probability that the 1st ball drawn is red = 4/11. The probability that the 2nd ball drawn is green = 5/10. The combined probability will then be 4/11 X 5/10 = 20/110 = 2/11.

39. B
(5-5) (1/2 – 3/7) = (7-6/14) = 1/14

40. D
-(-) becomes + and -(+) becomes -, therefore, -3 - (-7) - (+5) = -3 + 7 – 5, -4 + 5 = -1

41. D
First, convert all the terms to fractions and then cancel out. Therefore, 15/4 x 4/5 x 7/4 = 3/4 x 4/1 x 7/4, 3/4 x 1/1 x 7/1, 21/4 = 5 1/4

42. B
We see that there is a square with side 2 cm and a rectangle adjacent to it, with one side 2 cm (common side with the square) and the other side 4 cm. The perimeter of a shape is found by summing up all sides surrounding the shape, not adding the ones inside the shape. Three 2 cm sides from the square, and two 4 cm sides and one 2 cm side from the rectangle contribute the perimeter.

So, the perimeter of the shape is: 2 + 2 + 2 + 4 + 2 + 4 = 16 cm.

43. C
The sum of angles around a point is 360°
d + 300 = 360°
d = 60°

44. C
Pythagorean Theorem:
(Hypotenuse)^2 = (Perpendicular)^2 + (Base)^2
$h^2 = a^2 + b^2$

Given: $3^2 + 4^2 = h^2$
$h^2 = 9 + 16$
$h = \sqrt{25}$
h = 5

45. C
Large cube is made up of 8 smaller cubes of 5 cm sides.
Volume = Volume of small cube x 8
Volume = (5 x 5 x 5) x 8, 125 x 8
Volume = 1000 cm^3

What to Do After Taking a Practice Test

Steps for Maximizing Your Learning and Improvement

Taking a practice test is an excellent way to prepare for any exam, but it's just the beginning of the journey toward mastering the material. The real progress happens after the test when you review, analyze, and learn from your performance. Here are the steps you should take after completing a practice test:

Review Your Answers
Go through each question: Carefully check each question, whether you got it right or wrong. Understanding why you chose a particular answer is crucial to your learning.

Compare with the correct answers: Identify the correct answers and note where your understanding aligns or differs. This can help you pinpoint areas that need more attention.

Understand Your Mistakes
Analyze incorrect answers: For every wrong answer, figure out why it was incorrect. Was it due to a lack of knowledge, a misunderstanding of the question, or a simple mistake?
Identify patterns: Look for patterns in your mistakes. Are there specific topics or types of questions where you consistently struggle? Recognizing these patterns is key to targeted improvement.

Revisit the Material
Review related content: Go back to your textbooks, notes, or other study materials to review the topics that you found difficult. This reinforces your understanding and fills in any gaps.

Use additional resources: If needed, seek out additional resources such as online tutorials, videos, or study groups to gain a better grasp of the material.

Practice Similar Questions
Find similar questions: Practice more questions that are similar to the ones you got wrong. This helps solidify your understanding and improve your skills in those areas.

Use varied sources: Utilize different practice tests or question banks to get a wide range of questions and avoid memorizing answers.

Time Management
Assess your timing: Look at how long you took to complete the test and each question. Identify if there were any time sinks and think about how you can manage your time better in the future.

Practice under timed conditions: Simulate exam conditions by practicing under timed constraints. This helps you manage your time effectively and reduces anxiety during the actual test.

Time Management on a Test

https://www.test-preparation.ca/time-management/

Reflect on Your Strategy
Evaluate your approach: Reflect on the strategies you used during the test. Were there specific techniques that worked well or didn't work at all?

Adjust as needed: Based on your reflection, adjust your test-taking strategies. This might include better time management, different approaches to reading questions, or improved methods for eliminating incorrect answers.

Get Feedback
Ask for help: If possible, discuss your practice test with a teacher, tutor, or knowledgeable friend. They can provide valuable insights and explain difficult concepts.

Join study groups: Collaborate with peers who are also preparing for the same exam. Group study can offer new perspectives and shared resources.

Stay Consistent
Regular practice: Make practice tests a regular part of your study routine. Consistent practice helps you track your progress and keep your skills sharp.

Stay motivated: Keep your end goal in mind and remind yourself of the importance of your preparation. Celebrate small victories along the way to stay motivated.

Take Care of Yourself
Rest and recharge: Ensure you get enough rest and relaxation. Overworking can lead to burnout and reduce your effectiveness in studying.

Maintain a healthy lifestyle: Eat well, exercise regularly, and stay hydrated. A healthy body supports a sharp mind.

Super Foods for Studying
https://test-preparation.ca/super-foods-studying/

By following these steps, you'll not only improve your performance on practice tests but also enhance your overall understanding and confidence. Remember, practice tests are a tool for learning, not just assessment. Use them wisely, and you'll see significant progress on your path to success.

Conclusion

Congratulations! You have made it this far because you have applied yourself diligently to practicing for the exam and no doubt improved your potential score considerably! Getting into a good school is a huge step in a journey that might be challenging at times but will be many times more rewarding and fulfilling. That is why being prepared is so important.

Good Luck!

Register for Free Updates and More Practice Test Questions

Register your purchase at https://www.test-preparation.ca/register/ for fast and convenient access to updates, errata, free test tips and more practice test questions.

Online Resources

How to Prepare for a Test - The Ultimate Guide

https://www.test-preparation.ca/prepare-test/

Learning Styles - The Complete Guide

https://www.test-preparation.ca/learning-style/

Test Anxiety Secrets!

https://www.test-preparation.ca/test-anxiety/

Time Management on a Test

https://www.test-preparation.ca/time-management/

Flash Cards - The Complete Guide

https://www.test-preparation.ca/flash-cards/

How to Memorize - The Complete Guide

https://www.test-preparation.ca/memorize/

Super Foods for Studying

https://test-preparation.ca/super-foods-studying/

www.ingramcontent.com/pod-product-compliance
Lightning Source LLC
Chambersburg PA
CBHW081356070526
44583CB00020B/2573